Browsers, Devices, & Fonts

A designer's
guide to
fonts and
how they
function on
the web

*Gary
Rozanc*

Browsers, Devices, & Fonts

A Designer's Guide to Fonts and How They Function on the Web

Gary Rozanc

CRC Press
Taylor & Francis Group
Boca Raton London New York

CRC Press is an imprint of the
Taylor & Francis Group, an **informa** business

CRC Press
Taylor & Francis Group
6000 Broken Sound Parkway NW, Suite 300
Boca Raton, FL 33487-2742

Printed on acid-free paper
Version Date: 20181031

International Standard Book Number-13: 978-1-138-61231-0 (Paperback)
International Standard Book Number-13: 978-1-138-61234-1 (Hardback)

Visit the Taylor & Francis Web site at
http://www.taylorandfrancis.com

and the CRC Press Web site at
http://www.crcpress.com

Table of Contents

Author Bio

Gary Rozanc researches the best practices for teaching interactive and user experience design, specifically finding the ideal balance of visual design, user experience, and front-end development skills for the emerging interactive designer. To support his research, in May 2014, Gary's proposal "Web Designer Competencies Inventory and Recommendations for Inclusion in Design Curricula" was awarded the AIGA DEC Design Faculty Research Grant.

This research evolved into interviews with design practitioners to determine, contextualize, and prioritize these competencies, and is distributed via Gary's award winning podcast series *Design Edu Today*. Nationally recognized by the AIGA Design Educators Community, Design Incubation, and UCDA, *Design Edu Today* contributes to discovering the ideal balance between design disciplines that he brings back to the classroom.

Gary presents his research at international and national peer-reviewed conferences including AIGA's bi-annual National Conference "Head, Heart, Hand" and the "International Conference on Design Principles & Practices." Gary is an Assistant Professor in the Department of Visual Arts at the University of Maryland, Baltimore County, and received his BA with a concentration in graphic design from Cleveland State University, and his MFA in visual communications from the University of Arizona.

1 Introduction

While most designers I know obsess about typography, branding, and other forms of making, you will find me obsessing about determining the perfect balance of design and design-related disciplines ranging from front-end development (HTML and CSS) to user research, with a sprinkle of good old fashioned, hands-on skills like illustration to prepare my students to be highly sought after once they enter the industry. While my designer friends are practicing hand lettering or doing the 100 Day UI challenge in their spare time, I fill my notebooks and computer with ideas on how to perfect the balance of visual design, user experience design, and front-end development within a class, a series of classes, or an entire graphic design program. Unfortunately, this passion doesn't make for a super exciting notebook or online portfolio.

With all this pondering on creating a curriculum to prepare the perfect entry-level interactive designer, there is one specific set of skills I couldn't get a handle on—visual design vs. front-end development. Visual design refers to the study and creation of how something looks regardless of medium. This could be a company's logo, a navigation menu on a website, or a poster for a rock band. Front-end development is the execution of screen-based visual designs with HTML, CSS, and JavaScript. How do we combine these disciplines? Should designers code and should developers design? My answer to these questions has always been an unequivocal yes! As an interactive designer, you need to know how the medium you are designing for works to get the most out of it and avoid mistakes. Front-end developers need to know basic visual design principles as well, or what they create, while technically proficient, may be visually difficult for the audience to use.

I've spent the better part of four years trying to create the perfect balance between visual design and front-end development training for my aspiring interactive designers. I've tried teaching my students a front-end development heavy curriculum, but by the time they were proficient enough to make something to visually critique the semester was over. Plus, they'd forget everything I taught them and come back a semester or two later asking how to create something again since they didn't practice front-end development regularly once the class was over. I even created the bi-weekly podcast *Design Edu Today* where I interview experts involved in the interactive design process in hopes of getting them to define the perfect balance of visual design and front-end development. Alas, no such concrete information was forthcoming.

However, through these conversations I learned that all facets of interactive design are tested in a browser, on multiple devices before a website or an app goes live to the end user. This commonality made perfect sense to me when I put it into a print design context. Whether I was designing a poster, catalogue, or business card I would always print the design piece at actual size to identify any issues before I sent it off to the commercial printer. Checking a website or app during the development phase, before it goes live is no different than printing out your designs before they get into the customer's hands. You want to find issues early, before the end user does.

Exactly when the testing of the partially or fully developed design took place during the interactive design process varied wildly from guest to guest on the podcast. Over time, I discovered a trend within the timing of the testing during the interactive design process. Interactive firms that have visual designers and front-end developers under the same roof would conduct the testing almost immediately. In a gross oversimplification of the Agile Design Process, visual designers and front-end developers collaborate so visual design choices that don't work on devices or front-end development choices that adversely affect the visual design are identified before a site gets deep into production or goes live. This process saves a lot of time and money because there aren't as many revisions and starting and stopping the project waiting on the other person to finish their job. Interactive firms or freelancers that didn't work in the same room, zip code, or hemisphere as the front-end developer had a much different working process. These visual designers would create static mockups or clickable prototypes, get them approved by the client, and then send them to the front-end developer to create a fully developed website or app.

In this scenario major problems would occur. For example, if there were issues with how the static designs looked once translated into code it would cost the interactive designer time and money to go back and forth with the remote front-end developer to get the live code to the state that the visual design intended. If there was no time and money left for revisions with the front-end developer, the visual designer is either going to pay out of pocket, do a lot of explaining, or lose the client. Once I was able to identify this common pressure point in the interactive design process for the many visual designers who don't get to work alongside a front-end developer the answer to "Should designers code?" became crystal clear. Yes, designers should most definitely code, and I've spent the last two years figuring out exactly how much is necessary for a designer to be able to successfully hand off clickable prototypes created in programs like Adobe Xd and InVision to minimize the amount of time and money spent going back and forth with the front-end developer. However, I've subsequently learned that the amount of front-end development knowledge necessary to fully evaluate a design in different browsers and on multiple devices is minuscule and accessible to anyone no matter where they self-identify on the technology spectrum. Remember, this is coming from someone who spent several years emphatically championing that it was necessary for interactive designers to learn all there is to know about HTML and CSS and have a general understanding of JavaScript to be a successful designer.

As a print designer I didn't need to be a commercial printer to know if the poster design on my screen was going to be visually effective for my intended audience. I just needed to see a low-fidelity printout of my design at actual size to determine if my layout and typographic choices were still effective at a much larger scale. And there it was, *scale*. No matter what type of designer you are, from Architect to Industrial, scale is a core principle of design. Designers of all stripes use scale to guide and filter the audience through essential information of the designed piece. With scale being so critical, designers will go to great lengths to create a mockup or prototype that is as close to scale as time and budget will allow to get the most accurate representation of the final designed pieces before it gets in the hands of the end users. This newly found realization about the importance of scale made me look critically at what components of an interactive design piece are affected by scale. It was the usual print design culprits such as the smaller a three-column layout got, the more squished the content in the columns got, or the smaller the font size the harder it became to read interactive designs. Even a website's perfor-mance can affect scale if a font or image takes too long to download by distorting column widths and hierarchy. Unfortunately, unlike print design where you have at most three scales to work with, one at screen size, one at actual printed size, and one at distance, with interactive design you have an infinite number of scales. An iPhone 5s is a drastically different scale than an iPhone 7 Plus, both of which are completely different in scale than an Amazon Kindle Fire, or the 13" MacBook Pro. All of the aforementioned devices are of an entirely different scale than the 17" Dell Inspiron, the massive 28" Microsoft Surface Studio, or the tiny Apple Watch. Yet, as an interactive designer your websites and apps will be viewed on most if not all of these devices.

It's this multi-device user reality that is the reason I originally had my students learn enough front-end development skills to get their visual designs in a browser. By viewing their design choices at scale early on in the design process, they could avoid design decisions that weren't appropriate, even though this came at the expense of focusing on visual design and involved a tremendous learning curve of a discipline not directly related to visual design theory. So instead of teaching my visual design students to be front-end developers, I'm now teaching them to be identifiers and developers of scale within the interactive design realm. By learn-ing to identify what components of an interactive design piece are most affected by change in scale such as grid systems, typographic hierarchy, and imagery, the number of front-end development skills a visual designer needs to create an inter-active design element for testing in the browser across multiple devices is greatly reduced to a manageable number that can be seamlessly incorporated into your current design workflow.

If you self-identify as someone who creates visual designs that will be viewed on a screen and don't have the luxury of working alongside a front-end developer, then this book is for you no matter your level of visual design experience. I'll help you identify key scale issues your designs will face as they inevitably are viewed across an infinite number of devices, along with enough front-end development skills including writing HTML and CSS and working with actual devices and device emulators to create working prototypes of elements within your visual designs to evaluate those design choices live in browsers, on real devices. What this book won't cover is how to develop an entire website, make you a front-end developer, teach a front-end developer the basics of design, or discuss how to pick great font-pairings and what design looks best for the intended audience. This book's sole purpose is to help you find visual design performance and scale problems in real-world context before you send your mockups and prototypes off to the front-end developer while learning the fewest front-end development skills possible.

2 How the Web Works

Before architects can design a building, they need to understand the materials they are working with. Architects need to know the physical limits of concrete, steel, and wood if they plan to design something that is structurally sound and provide a habitable space for the intended users. Print designers also greatly benefit from understanding the materials and methods they are working with. Offset printing creates a different tactile experience from silkscreen or letterpress printing.

Because of these differences in printing, choosing the right paper for the unique printing method will yield the best results for the end users. You aren't going to find many architects or print designers arguing that you don't need to understand the medium you are working with on a basic level.

Yet, the number of interactive designers who understand the medium of web are few and far between. You don't have to be a construction expert to be an architect, and you don't need to be a commercial printer to be a graphic designer. The same holds true for interactive designers; they don't have to be front-end developers to be successful, they just need to understand the medium enough to make informed design decisions. In this chapter you will learn how Web Browsers and Web Servers work, and how Hypertext Markup Language (HTML), Cascading Style Sheets (CSS), and JavaScript create visual experiences for your users. This basic understanding of the web as a medium will empower you to make informed decisions during the design phase, eliminating a lot of mistakes that are only discovered during development or when a site goes live!

Finding a Website's Location

There are a lot of different components and systems working independently of each other to make it possible for a web browser such as Google's Chrome to display the website you were looking for. Before I discuss the specifics of those components and systems, I think it's best to start the journey the same way the user of a website would, by entering the domain name of a website into a web browser. The domain name of a website isn't actually meant for the web browser or web server where the files are located, rather it's meant for the user. Just like it's easier for you to remember your friend's name than it is to remember your friend's entire postal address, domain names are just an easy way for you to locate the physical address of a website. However, since the domain name doesn't contain an actual physical address for a website, your web browser needs to look up the address in a directory. This is done much in the same way as you'd look up telephone numbers and addresses in a phone book before they went extinct.

Once you enter the domain name into the web browser, it performs a search for the domain name's Domain Name Server (DNS) record. When someone registers a domain name, the domain registrar has a DNS that stores information about that domain name such as who registered it, should registration information be public, when the registration expires **(Figure 2.1)**, and most importantly it stores an Internet Protocol (IP) address.

DOMAIN INFORMATION

Domain:	facebook.com
Registrar:	MarkMonitor Inc.
Registration Date:	1997-03-29
Expiration Date:	2025-03-29
Updated Date:	2016-11-29
Status:	clientDeleteProhibited
	clientTransferProhibited
	clientUpdateProhibited
	serverDeleteProhibited
	serverTransferProhibited
	serverUpdateProhibited
Name Servers:	a.ns.facebook.com
	b.ns.facebook.com

REGISTRANT CONTACT

Name:	Domain Administrator
Organization:	Facebook, Inc.
Street:	1601 Willow Road,

Figure 2.1

The IP address is the physical location of the internet connected computer (web server) where your HTML, CSS, JavaScript, and many other file types are located. Every computer that is connected to the internet has an IP address, and servers that host websites have unique static IP addresses that never change. So once the web browser locates the IP address that corresponds to the domain name you requested, it's ready to begin looking for your files. While this process makes it easier for the end user, it does add extra lookup and computing time to the process. While most likely not noticeable on fast internet connections, typing 31.13.91.36 (the IP address for facebook.com) into a browser would help deliver the site content faster because the browser doesn't have to make an additional call to a DNS server to look up the physical address corresponding to the facebook.com domain name since you are supplying the direct location of the web server.

Requesting the Files

Even though the web browser has found the location of the web server hosting your files, there are still many additional steps in the process to load content into your web browser. Much like an apartment building has multiple units within a single building, a web server has a single physical address, but hosts multiple websites. The web browser needs to look up the location of the files you are requesting on the web server and does this by reading a directory of sites hosted on the particular web server. However, this time the web browser isn't looking for the IP address, it's now looking for a set of instructions that correspond with the domain name the user originally entered in the browser. Once the domain name is found, the information is then passed along to the web browser. This information will include the physical location of the directory on the web server, how to deliver the files contained inside that directory, what to do if the requested file is not found (404 error), and most important, how to serve the content: encrypted or unencrypted.

If the files are to be served unencrypted, the web browser will begin to download the files directly from the web server and display a Uniform Resource Locator (URL) in your web browser that will either have a prefix of HTTP://, or no prefix at all and some sort of notification that the connection is not secure **(Figure 2.2)**.

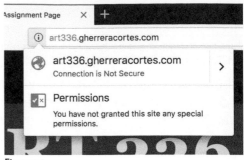

Figure 2.2

Now, if the files are to be delivered encrypted, there is an extra step in the process, the verification of the host of the files via a Secure Sockets Layer (SSL) certificate. In order to get the green "Secure Icon" **(Figure 2.3)** in the browser and a URL that starts with HTTPS:// the browser reads the SSL certificate located on the web server and then puts in a call to the SSL issu-

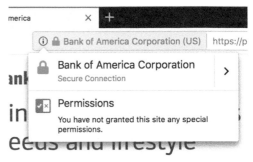

Figure 2.3

er such as VeriSign and GeoTrust to verify that the web server delivering the files is the same as the one listed in the certificate.This process also verifies the identity of the company that owns the web server through an extensive verification process much like a government background check.

If this Handshake (actual technical description) between the web server and the SSL issuer passes inspection, the web browser will begin to communicate with the web server to start the process of downloading files to the user's computer. However, if the handshake fails, the user will get a message from the web browser stating the content is not secure and that you

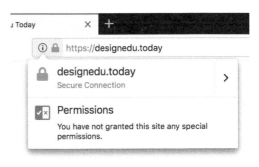

Figure 2.4

shouldn't proceed to visit the website. You may also see one other type of secure connection that doesn't list the company name, but rather just displays a green icon **(Figure 2.4)**. This type of SSL certificate only verifies that the server is delivering information over an encrypted connection; it does not verify the identity of the owner of the web server.

In the past, encrypted connections were typically used by online banking and eCommerce sites to ensure that the exchange of financial information entered by the user in the web browser and sent to the web server remained unreadable, even if it was intercepted by hackers, and verify the identity of the owner of the server. However, you will see more and more sites begin to use encryption for reasons beyond security. The most significant reason is Google has started to give search ranking priority to websites that deliver encrypted content. Organizations that are concerned with Search Engine Optimization (SEO) will make the switch to delivering encrypted content to improve their rankings, but many will forego the more involved SSL certification process that also verifies an organization's identity in favor of the simpler SSL certification process that only encrypts content.

Another design reason for SSL will be discussed in more detail later in this chapter, but briefly, the Hypertext Transfer Protocol (HTTP) has an updated version (referred to as HTTP/2) that delivers content to web browsers in a more streamlined manner that can boost the performance of a website. However, for HTTP/2 to be enabled on a web server and provide the performance increase, the connection needs to be encrypted. The increased performance will also help get a website higher in search engine rankings now that Google's search algorithm factors a site's performance into the rankings.

Delivering the Files

The following color scheme will be used to distinguish between HTML, CSS, and JavaScript throughout this chapter and the rest of the book.

```
CSS - Green
HTML - Orange
JavaScript - Purple
Terminal Commands - Blue
```

Once the web browser has found the location of the files on the web server and has identified whether to retrieve the files over an encrypted or unencrypted connection, it looks for instructions specific to the website about what content to deliver and how to handle the content. By default, the web browser will first look for a site's instructions and content in an "index" file. Index.htm, index.html, index.php, index.asp files all serve the same purpose: giving an initial set of instructions and location of content to the web browser. All HTML files contain two sections designated with the <head> and the <body> HTML tags that the browser will read. Most of the information about how the website will look (the presentation) is contained in the <head> and most of the content (the structure) such as images and text marked up with HTML are contained in the <body>. There is a third set of instructions that web browser will look for that can be written in a language such as JavaScript (the behavior). Depending on the behaviors being changed—features like image sliders, animated page scrolls, swipe gestures, and form alerts are examples of behaviors—the JavaScript instructions could be placed anywhere in the HTML file with the <script> tag.

Once the web browser starts reading the instructions it begins to download the additional assets listed in the HTML (index.html) file. These assets can include information in the form of external CSS and JavaScript files, .jpeg, .gif, or .png images, or fonts not already installed on the user's computer that will need to be downloaded by the web browser from the remote web server. It's also important to understand the two different ways the files can be downloaded by the web browser. Over an unencrypted HTTP connection each file that will be downloaded gets its own individual request from the web browser. In layman's terms, the web browser reads the HTML file until it finds something it needs to download, then makes a request to the web server to deliver that specific file. This would be a process similar to sending someone to the grocery store to do your shopping, but only telling them what you need purchased a single item at a time. Painstakingly, making them go back and forth multiple times—item by item—until everything on the list has been retrieved.

This is a very time-consuming process and front-end developers will stress that web sites served over this type of connection should be limited visually in the number of files—images and fonts—necessary to be downloaded to help speed up the site's performance. However, this bottleneck in the file retrieval process has been addressed in the new HTTP/2 specification. With HTTP/2, once the connection to the web server is open, it remains open. Using the grocery store analogy, an HTTP/2 approach gives the person doing the shopping the entire shopping list while at the store, so they can get everything on the list at once. While this may seem like a magic bullet, it does have its own caveats. One of the biggest is HTTP/2's adoption is not as widespread as you would think. Because you need to set up SSL certificates to use the new specification, it adds an extra step in the setup process that isn't as straightforward for non-developers and clients leaving many sites still being served over HTTP. It also requires a software update to the web server, which may not be possible on outdated operating systems. Because of this, you will need to be able to create visual designs for both delivery methods which will be discussed in the upcoming chapters.

Often overlooked by designers, a Content Delivery Network (CDN) is a method that a front-end developer might employ to speed up a website's performance. From a visual design perspective, a CDN isn't much different than a web server, it's a networked computer on the internet with its own set of DNS and internal server settings. However, what makes a CDN different and worth knowing about as a visual designer, is that it can speed up how long it takes for the web browser to download fonts, images, and other file types listed in the HTML file. The CDN speeds things up by having a global network of cloned servers that will deliver the requested file to your web browser from the server closest to your physical location. For example, if the HTML file sitting on a web server in New York City tells the user located in Chicago whose web browser is referencing the file to download a few images and a font, a CDN will deliver the requested files to the web browser from the CDN server nearest Chicago. Using the grocery store analogy again, this would be like living in Chicago and sending someone to fetch your groceries from a store in New York City, instead of the grocery store right down the street from where you live. The use of a CDN will definitely help the performance of a website and if the client or developer suggests you use one, you should follow the advice.

Rendering the Website

Now that the web browser has opened up a connection with the web server and has instructions and content to work with, the web browser will do one more critical test before it begins to render the site's content. With the introduction of CSS3, the @media rule was added to give web browsers the ability to detect many aspects of the viewing environment of the user, including the size of the viewable area of the open web browser window (viewport), and apply CSS rules based on specific size ranges defined by the designer or front-end developer. This feature has led to what is now referred to as "Responsive Web Design" where a single website will deliver a unique visual experience based on the environment of the end user **(Figures 2.5, 2.6 & 2.7)**.

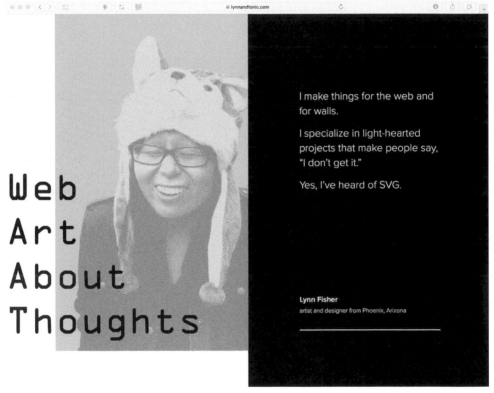

Figure 2.5

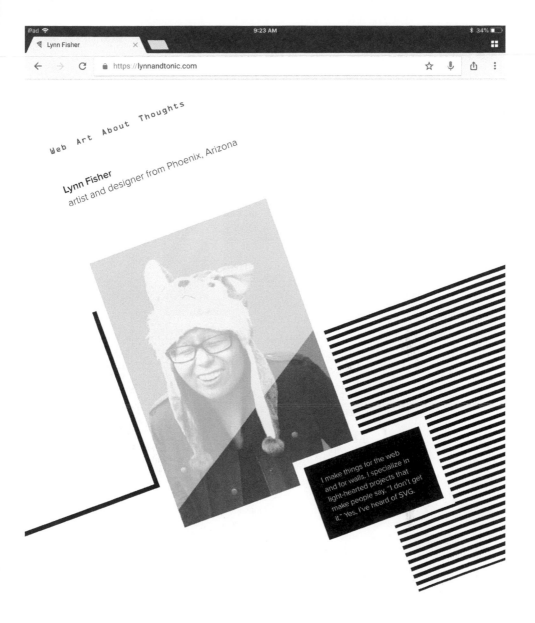

Figure 2.6

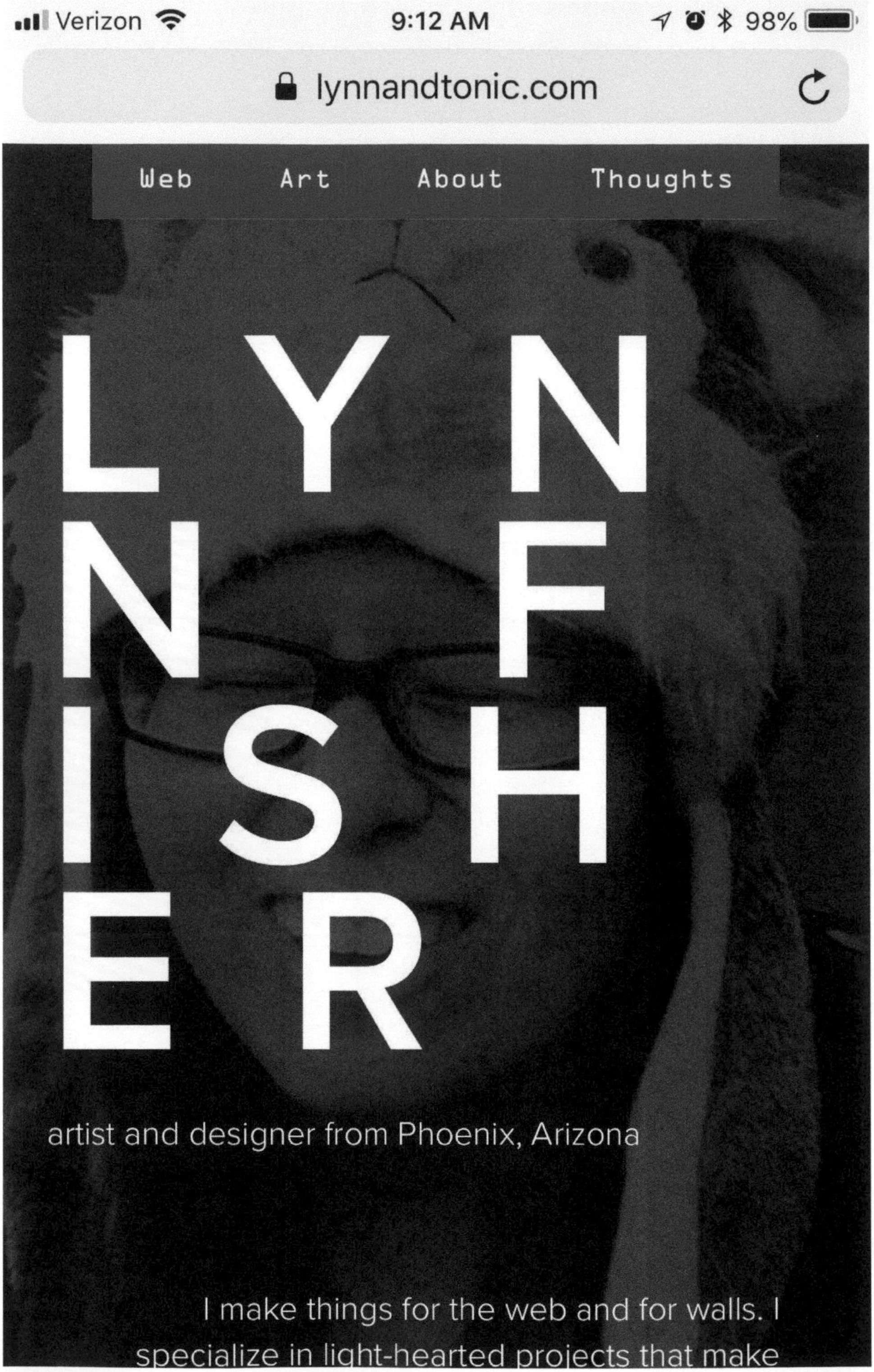

Verizon
9:12 AM
98%
lynnandtonic.com
Web
Art
About
Thoughts
LYN
N F
ISH
E R
artist and designer from Phoenix, Arizona
I make things for the web and for walls. I
specialize in light-hearted projects that make

Figure 2.7

Armed with the dimensions of the viewport, the web browser begins the rendering process to display the content of the HTML file on the screen: this will include all text and images contained within the `<body>` tag. As the web browser is displaying the content on the screen it is also reading all CSS instructions. The CSS instructions will give the web browser stylistic information such as font choice, background colors, column dimensions, grid layout, line spacing, and much, much more. Some of the CSS instructions will be specific to a viewport size, such as changing font sizes for optimal reading on different devices. Other CSS instructions will be more general such as color choices. If you are familiar with using Adobe's InDesign, CSS files are very similar to creating character, page, and paragraph styles to consistently control the visual appearance of the content from a single set of instructions. However, what makes Interactive Design different from Print Design is the final print piece has a fixed dimension unlike websites and apps that will be displayed on an infinite number of differently sized devices.

As the web browser is displaying the contents of the HTML file and applying the rules declared in the CSS file, the web browser is also reading the behavior changing information such as JavaScript files. In an oversimplification of the process, JavaScript can interrupt or change the default behavior of the HTML file and the CSS declarations. For example, image sliders or carousels only show one image at a time and rely on a mouse click or swipe movement to advance to the next image. There currently is no default behavior in HTML or CSS that would make a swipe motion on a touch screen trigger a carousel to advance to the next image. To add this behavior, JavaScript instructions are written to let the browser know that if someone swipes the image, the next or previous image in the series should be displayed. Another example is audio and video players. Currently, you are very limited how you can visually style the default HTML media player with CSS. With the use of JavaScript, you gain the ability to style a player with CSS to your heart's content. There are a great many other examples of what can be done with JavaScript, but for the purpose of this book and visual designers, JavaScript adds features not possible through native HTML and CSS, but without proper care and implementation, JavaScript can greatly reduce a web site's performance. Even worse, if the end user has disabled JavaScript, the website could be completely unusable, so when asking a front-end developer to change default behaviors do so with caution.

Another key element to consider when creating your visual designs is Render Blocking. This is a very literal term where certain CSS and JavaScript instructions prevent the website from being rendered by the web browser while it waits for the render blocking files to be downloaded. One example of render blocking that will be covered in detail in later chapters is the use of web fonts. The CSS used to instruct the web browser to download and then display the site's content using the font is render blocking. This is why you sometimes see text displayed in a default system font like Arial or Times suddenly change to a different custom font or the site appears to have no text at all and then suddenly the text flashes in. In extreme cases of render blocking, improper use of JavaScript can actually cause a website to never render at all, giving the user a blank screen to look at. While avoiding or minimizing render blocking is the realm of the front-end developer, as a visual designer there are aspects of this you can control that will be covered in Chapter 04 *Typography,* but remember visual design choices you make can affect a web browser's ability to display a site's content in a timely manner.

Now, once the web browser has loaded the content listed in the HTML file, applied the CSS instructions (declarations), and changed or added any behaviors via JavaScript, the website is fully rendered in the browser and on your screen. With a well-designed and coded website, this process can appear to start to happen within a second. Once a website's design gets bloated with multiple images, web fonts, and behavior changes, etc., it can take much longer for a website to appear in your browser. This can be very unfortunate for the website's owner. There are extensive studies[1,2] that demonstrate users will abandon a website if they don't perceive that the site will give them what they are looking for within two seconds and be ready to abandon a site after only a second. Users on mobile devices are a bit more forgiving, but not by much. Mobile users will start abandoning a site after three seconds. This is why it's so critical for designers to understand the medium of the web. Without this understanding, the visual design of a website can drive users away in droves.

Final Thoughts

While there is a lot going on behind the scenes of making a website appear on your screen, a lot of which is out of your control, smart visual design choices can make performant websites the users will love. Throughout the remaining chapters of this book, you will learn how to identify if your design choices will become a bottleneck in the process. You will also learn visual design strategies that take advantage of the web browser's rendering process, so it's important to know what's really happening when you first enter a website's URL.

---

1   Wired.com. 2014. Great Expectations: 47% of Consumers Want a Web Page to Load in 2 Seconds or Less. http://insights.wired.com/profiles/blogs/47-of-consumers-expect-a-web-page-to-load-in-2-seconds-or-less/ (accessed April 22, 2018).

2   Eaton, Kit. 2012. How One Second Could Cost Amazon $1.6 Billion In Sales. https://www.fastcompany.com/1825005/how-one-second-could-cost-amazon-16-billion-sales (accessed April 21, 2018).

3 Setting Up Your Toolbox

As I've previously mentioned I'm a design educator. Rest assured I've spent more time agonizing over the best sequence to introduce the contents of this book to you in the most organic way possible. Probably way more time than was physically or emotionally necessary. For instance, I have spent an enormous amount of time and thought energy trying to figure out whether *Testing* or *Evaluating* is the best word to describe the process this book will teach you.

I prefer the word testing, but it sounds scary. Evaluating isn't nearly as scary, but sometimes you will actually run a test, then evaluate the results of the test.

So, pardon the Gollum like personality switch between the two terms that will occur throughout the book. Also, I'm not saying that tongue-in-cheek or to be witty, rather the process I am going to demonstrate for you throughout this book falls into the "What came first? The chicken or the egg?" conundrum. You will need to have a physical example in front of you to be able to learn to evaluate it for scale, but in order for you to have something to evaluate, you need to be able to create it. Since there is circular logic at work here, I decided to move forward with the idea that you

01. Set up your working environment.
02. Create the visual design elements so they can be seen in browsers and devices.
03. Test and evaluate your visual design choices.

Since this is the method I thought best for this book, you will see a lot of references in demos to work that you just created, and fewer examples of outside work and how to evaluate existing outside work. By design, upon completion of the demos and readings in this book you will determine for yourself that the process I introduced is not linear and you will be able to apply any part of it suit your own needs in the future.

What You Are Going to Need

Now, as I just mentioned you will need to create visual design elements for the browser before you can test or evaluate it to make your informed design decisions. To be able to create interactive design elements to test in the browsers and on devices you will need some new tools. You will need to sign up for some free online tools, potentially pay for a couple of subscriptions to different online tools, or install open source software on your computer in non-traditional ways to avoid paying for a subscription. All of the different options will be discussed in-depth and I'll discuss the pros and cons of each.

Gathering Browsers and Devices

Since you are going to be evaluating your designs choices in the browser, you are going to need browsers, as in multiple browsers! Here is a partial list of the ones you should be testing in based on general usage statistics for the United States. You can check out stats for specific countries and regions at StatCounter.com.[1] You will need the macOS and Windows versions as well as the Android and iOS versions of the following.

- Chrome 47.96%

- Safari 31.63%

- Internet Explorer 6.01%

- Firefox 5.36%

- Edge 3.95%

- Opera 0.5%

Downloading the browsers is the most straightforward part of the gathering browsers and devices process. Figuring out what types of devices you should be evaluating your design choices on is much more subjective. There are tons of studies that break down what types of devices are most frequently used on the world's most popular websites.[2] There are even a few books dedicated to helping you create device labs.[3] Depending on where you live, you may have access to an Open Device Lab.[4] For the sake of this book and staying true to what we need to do as visual designers to properly evaluate your design choices—while it's nice to have access to—you don't need to own a front-end development level device lab like thunder::tech's[5] User Experience Lab[6] **(Figure 3.1)**. Instead you should first focus on what you already have, what you can easily get, and then round out your collection with low-cost devices that add variety in size and operating system.

---

1   StatCounter. 2018. Browser Market Share United States Of America. http://gs.statcounter.com/browser-market-share/all/united-states-of-america (accessed July 20, 2018).

2   W3 Schools. 2018. Browser Statistics. https://www.w3schools.com/browsers/default.asp (accessed April 21, 2018).

3   Hogan, Lara, and Montague, Destiny. 2015. Building a Device Lab. http://buildingadevicelab.com/ (accessed April 21, 2018).

4   Open Device Labs. 2018. Find the right Open Device Lab for your mission and location. https://opendevicelab.com/ (accessed April 21, 2018).

5   thunder::tech. 2018. Digital Marketing Agency & Web Design Firm. https://www.thundertech.com/ (accessed April 21, 2018).

6   thunder::tech. 2018. User Experience Lab. http://uxlab.thundertech.com/ (accessed April 21, 2018).

The User Experience Lab at thunder::tech. Cleveland, Ohio.

Figure 3.1

First, start with your existing devices; this will be your base from which to build upon. For example, I have an Apple iPhone 7 Plus and an iPad 2 that I use every day. I also hung on to my old iPhone 4s instead of selling it. So right there, operating system aside, I have three very uniquely sized devices to evaluate designs on. Since my iPhone 4s is pretty small and my iPhone 7 Plus is really big I decided to start rounding out my collection my getting devices that used different operating systems in sizes I don't already have. My local Radio Shack was closing so I went to their liquidation sale once it hit 50% off storewide and got a prepaid LG Tribute running Android for about $50.00 that I didn't activate. The LG Tribute is bigger than the iPhone 4s and smaller than the iPhone 7 Plus, so this gave me a good balance in size. Now that I had a decent enough variation in sizes I looked for the cheapest prepaid Windows phone I could find. I ended up with a NOKIA Lumina 635 running Windows 8 off of Amazon for about $40.00.

Now that I felt that I had a decent collection of smartphones that ranged in size and covered most of the popular operating systems I decided to focus on tablet devices. Since my iPad 2 is fairly big, and anything bigger would start to mimic the screen size of a small laptop I started looking for smaller tablet devices. Looking at my collection as a whole **(Figure 3.2)**, I saw that I was missing three different operating systems, Amazon, Blackberry, and Windows 10, so that lead me to getting a 7" Amazon Fire tablet when they went on sale for $39.99 which also filled the size gap between my iPhone 7 Plus and the iPad 2.

Figure 3.2

Finally, I'm privileged to have both a 12" MacBook and a 27" iMac to round out my collection. I can't stress enough how essential having the 27" monitor is for evaluating designs. The typographic scale varies wildly between the 12" MacBook and the 27" iMac so I'd suggest looking into getting an inexpensive 27" monitor from Acer or Dell if you don't already have one. Yes, it may be a luxury, but you'd be shocked at how different your design choices look on a 27" inch screen compared to a 12", 13", or even 15" screen.

I'm not trying to tell you that you need the exact devices that I have. There is no perfect solution other than owning every single device known to humankind. Since that's not possible, you want a set of devices that represents a wide range of sizes and popular operating systems. To this day I am still on the lookout for a super cheap tablet that runs the Android operating system and anything Blackberry. I frequently check eBay and Groupon Goods for deals and one day when I have some discretionary income that coincides with a good deal on one of those devices I'll pull the trigger and get one. Another good source of devices is your friends and family. Ask them to give you their old devices instead of selling them or trading them in. Finally, I'm always on the lookout for a super cheap Windows 10 device so I can evaluate my designs in Microsoft's Edge browser. Until I finally get one, I'm stuck using an emulator which I will also cover later in the book.

Since you are going to be evaluating your designs in each of these browsers, I suggest in addition to installing Chrome, Edge, Firefox, Internet Explorer, Opera, and

Safari, you want to install a QR reader app. You will use the QR Reader to quickly open up browser tabs you have on your laptop or desktop on your mobile devices. You will also want to get a QR code creator for each of the browsers you installed. This generates a QR code in a popup window of the URL you are currently viewing on a laptop or desktop computer, so you can quickly scan it into your mobile devices, saving yourself a lot of typing. I've listed the QR code generators I'm using for my own setup.

- Chrome: The QR Code Extension https://chrome.google.com/webstore/detail/the-qr-code-extension/oijdcdmnjjgnnhgljmhkjlablaejfeeb

- Firefox: QR Code Image https://addons.mozilla.org/en-US/firefox/addon/generate-qr-code/?src=api

- Opera: QR Box https://addons.opera.com/en/extensions/details/qr-box/?display=en

- Safari: QRify https://safari-extensions.apple.com/details/?id=de.retiolum.safari.qrify-RSADU6MKX9

General Resources and Subscriptions

When it comes to getting your visual design choices in the browser, there are multiple ways to achieve that which will be discussed shortly. However, no matter your preferred working method, you will need to either sign up for or download each of the following. Now, before you do, I'll let you know upfront that you won't need access to this all at once and I'll give you reminders at the beginning of each demonstration when you will actually need them. Don't worry if you don't understand what any of these links are for just yet. I promise we will be covering it in detail when appropriate to the demo. Again, this is a Chicken vs. Egg conundrum. Do I discuss what they are going to be needed for before we need them or as soon as we need them? I'm going with the idea of let's gather supplies first with general descriptions then discuss in-depth when necessary for a demonstration. This is basically a list for you to reference after you have finished the book and don't want to rely on your memory to find the exact chapter where I referenced the resource. The resources listed are in no particular order.

- You will need to access quite a few resources on CodePen at https://codepen.io/browsersdevicesfonts so keep it handy!

- You will need an Adobe Typekit https://typekit.com account. If you are a subscriber to Adobe Creative Cloud, Typekit is included with your subscription. If you aren't an Adobe Creative Cloud subscriber, there is a subscription model with a free tier that will serve the needs of this book.

- Google Fonts is another resource you will want to keep handy. https://fonts.google.com/

- You should also keep The League of Moveable Type's URL handy https://www.theleagueofmoveabletype.com/. You'll be needing it to learn how to use self-hosted fonts in your evaluations and tests.

What You Need for a Browser Based Workflow

If you want to evaluate your design choices in a browser across multiple devices you are going to need a text editor to write the necessary, but minimal, amount of HTML and CSS. To write your HTML and CSS a free account at CodePen http://codepen.io/ will be all that you need to do *most* of your design evaluations (notice I didn't say testing). Now, there are some pros and cons to this workflow, but there isn't a perfect workflow. You just need to pick the workflow that is most comfortable for you to incorporate into your daily design practice.

Pros
- CodePen is free.

- Testing on CodePen with a device emulator is free!

- There is no software setup.

- It's operating system independent.

- It reduces the amount of HTML and CSS you need to learn.

- With a paid Pro subscription this will be all that you need for evaluating and testing purposes.

Cons
- You need internet access to use this workflow.

- If your office is behind a security firewall, you may not be able to access the site.

- Unless you pay for a Pro subscription, there are some key evaluations and tests you can't perform with your typography and imagery.

Getting to Know CodePen, CodePen Pro, & Device Emulators

If you are going to use the Browser Based workflow you will primarily be working in CodePen. CodePen is an online editor that displays the results of your work in real time, while nearly eliminating the need for file management that is quite finicky for those unfamiliar with HTML and CSS. CodePen has another huge benefit, it has partnered with CrossBrowserTesting to let you test your pens on a device emulator. While not a replacement for real devices, the emulator will give you an approximation of what your design choices will look like across operating systems and browsers, avoiding possible issues with client expectations. CodePen's basic features are free, and that's primarily what you will need for the demonstrations in this book.

In the chapters where you evaluate the performance of your self-hosted typographic choices and experiment with images, you will either need to switch to the Native Application based workflow, or subscribe to CodePen Pro. There is a 14-day free trial of CodePen Pro, so I'd suggest waiting untill you get to the point in Chapter 4 when you will first need the feature before starting the free Pro trial. Depending on your pace, the 14 days may give you enough time to determine if the subscription is right for you. Keep in mind CodePen Pro has both a yearly and monthly subscription rate. A single month at the monthly subscription rate for Pro will give you enough time to determine if the Browser based workflow is right for you before signing up for the reduced yearly subscription rate.

There is already a lot of documentation on how to use CodePen, CodePen Pro, and CrossBrowserTesting. If you decide to use the Browser based workflow, I'd highly recommend taking the time to go more in-depth on how to use these tools. There are a lot of features and steps available to speed up your working process. For the sake of this book however, I'm only going to cover the basic features you will need to evaluate your design choices outlined in this book.

HOW TO FORK A PEN

Eventually you may want to create a new pen from scratch as you become more familiar with HTML, CSS, and front-end development techniques. However, you'll be able to do all the evaluations by simply copying (forking) an existing pen I created for you. The actual links to the pen you will need to copying (forking) for specific exercises will be given when demonstrated in a particular section within a chapter. The following link is simply for demonstration purposes on how to fork a pen.

01. The first thing you will need to do is sign up for a free CodePen account at https://codepen.io. Once you've signed up for the free account, make sure you are still logged in. This will ensure that forked pens stay in your account.

02. Next, enter the URL https://codepen.io/browsersdevicesfonts/pen/rvOLxw, or you could browse the pens at https://codepen.io/browsersdevicesfonts/pens/public/ that I created for this book and search for the pen titled "Getting Started" **(Figure 3.3)**.

03. Once you have the "Getting Started" pen open, click the "Fork" button across the top of the screen.

Figure 3.3

Tip

For exercises in future chapters, make a habit of forking the pen to make a copy of it in your pen library, then fork the pen again and work from the newly created pen. This method creates a base or template pen for you to work from within your own library. As you proceed through this book adding evaluation and testing techniques to your work-flow, it will be nice to have a base pen to start from within your own account.

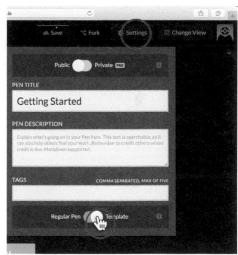

Figure 3.4

You can formalize this process by turning a pen into an actual template **(Figures 3.4, 3.5, & 3.6)**. This process makes it easier for you to create new pens based on a saved template. The free account lets you create 3 templates; the Pro subscription gives you unlimited templates.

Figure 3.5   Figure 3.6

HOW TO WORK IN YOUR PENS

Now that you have forked the "Getting Started" pen to get it into your library, you can either fork it again (best practice for your daily design workflow) or continue to work in this pen since you won't need it after this basic demonstration. Before you start any editing in your newly created/forked pen, rename it. By default, it will label a new pen as "Untitled" or keep the name of the forked pen, making it difficult to find what you are looking for once you start working. For this demonstration I have renamed the forked pen to "Changing Background Color" **(Figures 3.7 & 3.8)**.

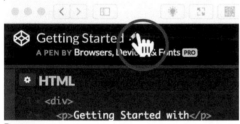

Figure 3.7   Figure 3.8

For the purposes of this book, you won't be needing to edit or write any JavaScript. Fortunately, CodePen makes it easy to open and close any of the three editing panels. Simply click and drag on the divider **(Figure 3.9)**.

Figure 3.9

Now that you collapsed the JavaScript panel and are left with the HTML and CSS panels you can begin to edit their contents. It's a really straight-forward process, very similar to using Google Docs, or any other online text editor. To practice editing, find line 2 in the HTML panel and replace the words "Getting Started" with the new title "Changing a Background Color." As you are doing this, pay attention to the preview panel as your edits are displayed in real time. Ignoring the commenting in the CSS panel telling you not to delete or change anything below this line, look for and change `background-color: #262626;` to `background-color: rebeccapurple;`[7] and note the change you see **(Figures 3.10 & 3.11)**.

Figure 3.10

Figure 3.11

Finally, there will come a time when you will rather see your pens fill the entire page, without any editor panels open. To do this, simply click on the "Change View" button across the top and select "Full Page" from the dropdown menu **(Figure 3.12)**. If you haven't already verified your email address with CodePen, you may see an error that won't let you use the "Change View" feature until you do.

Figure 3.12

If you happen to get a message asking if you want to "Stay on Page" or "Leave Page," click "Stay on Page" and then click on the "Save" button **(Figure 3.13)**. This will save the changes you made to the pen and allow you to exit to the full-page view. While CodePen can be set up to auto save changes, when you try to leave an unsaved pen, you will most likely see the same "Stay on Page" or "Leave Page" message.

Figure 3.13

---

7   Meyer, Eric. 2014. rebeccapurple. https://meyerweb.com/eric/thoughts/2014/06/19/rebeccapurple/ (accessed April 21, 2018).

After clicking the "Save" button you will be able to repeat the change view process and see your pen in the full browser window **(Figure 3.14)**.

Figure 3.14

HOW TO DOWNLOAD ASSETS

At its core, CodePen is just a web browser with a built-in text editor that refreshes the web page in real time, but behind the scenes it does a lot to make the evaluating and testing process a lot easier for you. The downside to all that automation is that it makes it harder for your to do performance testing. However, there is a very simple workaround for this. CodePen gives you the ability to export the files it creates for you. The exported files don't contain any of the editing features of CodePen which will allow you to evaluate and test your

Figure 3.15

designs for performance. To export your pen as raw HTML and CSS files simply click on the "Export" button on the bottom of the screen and then click on the "Export .zip" option to begin the download **(Figure 3.15)**.

Depending on your browser settings, you will either get a folder or a .zip file with the name of your pen in lowercase, with hyphens replacing blank spaces. Inside the unzipped folder you will see a few different files and subfolders. To help you make sense of everything, the index.html file is the contents of the HTML panel in CodePen, and the styles.css is the contents of the CSS panel. If you were to double click the index.html file, it would launch your default web browser and open up in "Full Page" view. CodePen's ability to create and organize files behind the scenes is one of the advantages of using the Browser based workflow. If you are using the Native Application based workflow, you will have to manage this process yourself. It's not complicated, but it is an extra step.

HOW TO USE CROSSBROWSERTESTING

As I have already discussed, you will need devices to evaluate and test your designs in future chapters. Until you build up a suitable device lab, you can take advantage of CodePen's partnership with the CrossBrowserTesting service. CrossBrowserTesting will give you a simulation of what your pen would look like on a wide array of devices and operating systems, from laptops running Windows through all the different versions of iPhones. This is another perk of using the Browser based workflow, unless you test directly from CodePen, device emulation services similar to CrossBrowserTesting cost a minimum of $20.00 or more a month!

CodePen makes it pretty easy to get started. All you need to do is click on the "Change View" button and then click on the "Open on CrossBrowserTesting" link in the dropdown menu **(Figure 3.16)**. This should open a new tab and prompt you to login to CrossBrowserTesting's website. Most likely, you haven't signed up for a free account yet, so take the time and do that now. If you aren't redirected back to the device emulation page with a link to your CodePen page after you sign up for a free account, simply go back to your pen and start the process over, logging in with your newly created credentials.

Figure 3.16

Once you are logged in, you will see a page with a bunch of different buttons, tabs, and options. No matter which device you own to design, evaluate, and test your designs on, you need to be testing on the devices you don't have based on the most up-to-date statistics on browser usage. However, ideally you would work with your client to obtain the analytics of their current website which will give you the list of all the browsers, devices, and operating systems that site visitors commonly use. You should be checking your designs on the most popular devices based on the analytics from actual users **(Figure 3.17)**.

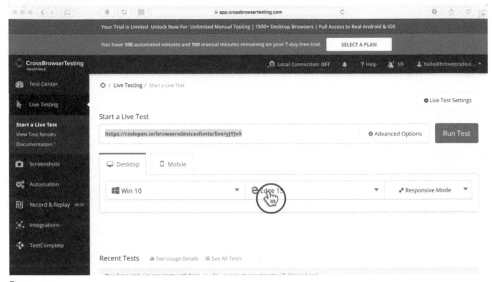

Figure 3.17

You can change the type of devices by clicking on the "Desktop" and "Mobile Tabs," and you can change operating system, browser, and screen resolution by clicking on the dropdown menus. If for some reason you can't select the options I just mentioned, select the oldest browser and operating system combination CrossBrowserTesting will allow **(Figures 3.18 & 3.19)**.

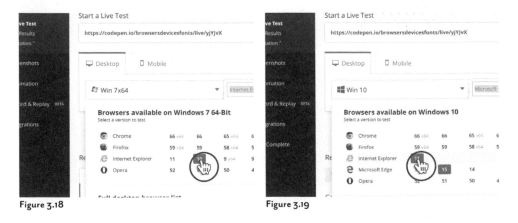

Figure 3.18   Figure 3.19

Once you've selected the device you want to emulate, if the URL to the pen you are working on isn't pre-populated into the "Start a Live Test" input field, copy and paste the URL from your open pen into the field and click "Run Test" **(Figure 3.20)**. It may take a few seconds for the emulation to load, but once it does, you will see your pen emulated in the browser of choice.

Tips

The embedded browser window is scrollable. If your designs are too long to be seen in the entire browser window at once, you can scroll to evaluate the entire

Figure 3.20

length of your design. You may not notice right away, especially if you didn't pick the exact operating system and browser versions as I did, the text has jumped to the top and is no longer in the center of the screen **(Figure 3.21)**. It's for this exact reason that you need to evaluate and test your web designs on real devices or at the very least, emulators. As HTML, CSS, and JavaScript mature, browsers continually update to add support for new features. The pen was tested in Internet Explorer 10, but partial support for CSS Grid didn't come until Internet Explorer 11 with full support only coming to Microsoft's Edge 16 **(Figure 3.21)**.

Figure 3.21

You may also notice that you have a white screen **(Figure 3.22)** with the purple background color missing! Internet Explorer 10 was released on September 4, 2012, but the color rebeccapurple wasn't added to the CSS specification until June 14, 2014, in honor of the passing of Rebecca Alison Meyer. Since the color didn't exist in the CSS specification in 2012, the web browser won't display it. While CSS background colors are generally not written as names, rather as hexadecimal values that all browsers can render regardless of how old, there are many modern HTML and CSS features that browsers don't yet support. So, it's imperative to make sure critical design choices work on the devices the audience will be using to access your site.

Figure 3.22

It's important to note that testing for HTML and CSS features generally falls under the realm of the front-end developer. You will be supplying the developer with some sort of prototype that becomes a visual blueprint for them to build the site from. However, it's important for visual designers to learn the medium of HTML and CSS—warts and all—to become better, more strategic designers. This is just one small example of why understanding the medium is beneficial, though not detrimental if you don't.

HOW TO MANAGE ASSETS

Having the ability to host assets such as images and fonts within CodePen eliminates the need for the Native Application workflow method, so it's worth considering. However, this feature is only available to CodePen Pro subscribers. If you are relying on the 14-day free trial to determine if you are going to pay for a subscription, I recommend that you skip this section. When you finally start using this feature in Chapter 04 *Typography*, you will be prompted to come back here to learn how to manage assets. To get started, all you need to do to upload an asset is click on the "Asset" button located across the bottom of the screen.

Clicking on the "Asset" button **(Figure 3.23)** will open a Design Assets management window. From here you can see your files, copy the links to those files, and upload new files. By clicking on the "Choose Files" button **(Figure 3.24)**, a file upload dialogue box will open up and you can upload your fonts, images, and other assets.

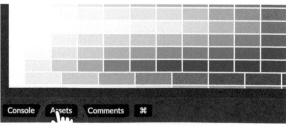

Figure 3.23

Figure 3.24

Figure 3.25

Once your file is finished uploading, you will be able to copy the link or path to the file **(Figure 3.25)**. You will use this link in the HTML and CSS editor panels to load files necessary for accurate evaluation and testing.

In this example you can see the code I copied and pasted into the CSS panel to make the image appear as a background **(Figure 3.26)**. By having CodePen Pro host my assets, I can do all the necessary evaluation and testing from a single program, streamlining my workflow significantly. You should upload your own image (file must be under 2MB) and copy and paste the code into the CSS panel like I demonstrated. Doing this will help you get used to the interface.

Figure 3.26

After you've uploaded your assets, you may want to delete them, rename them, etc. Fortunately, there is an Asset Manager built into CodePen Pro that can do all that. To access the Asset Manager, click on the profile icon to open up the menu and then click on the "Asset Manager" link **(Figure 3.27)**. Once you are in the Asset Manager you can click on an asset name to open its preview **(Figure 3.28)**.

The Asset Manager defaults to displaying image assets **(Figure 3.29)**. If you need to access the fonts you'll be uploading, click on the "Other" tab **(Figure 3.30)**. The Asset Manager won't give you a preview of your uploaded fonts, but you will still be able to copy the URL, delete, and rename it.

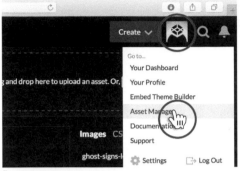

Figure 3.27

Figure 3.28

Figure 3.29

Figure 3.30

What You Need for a Native Application Based Workflow

Just like with the Browser based workflow, your goal is to be able to write HTML and CSS to get your design choices in a browser to view them on different devices. To accomplish all of this you will need to download and install Brackets http://brackets.io/ and BrowserSync https://www.browsersync.io. I picked these two programs because they are open source, operating system independent, and have a very active development community. That said, there are other pieces of software that do the same thing if the ones I'm mentioning here were to ever go away, such as CodeKit (macOS) and Prepros (macOS and Windows) so you don't have to worry about this process ever becoming obsolete.

Pros

- It's free.

- It's operating system independent.

- You will be able to do all your evaluations and tests with one workflow.

Cons

- It's not as easy to set up.

- You will need to learn to not be scared of the command line.

- You will need to learn a little extra HTML and CSS.

- If you don't have a Wi-Fi network setup already, you'll need to make an ad-hoc one.

- You'll need to pay for a subscription to a device emulator if you don't have a robust device lab!

INSTALLING BRACKETS

With the Native Application based workflow, you will need a text editor to write your HTML and CSS files in place of the CodePen editor. Brackets is an open source text editor available on both macOS and Windows operating systems that will handle everything you will need for this book, and more **(Figure 3.31)**! The installation of brackets is straightforward; simply go to http://brackets.io/ and click on the "Download Brackets" button.

Figure 3.31

Once the download has finished on macOS, double click the .dmg file and in the ensuing dialogue box drag the Brackets application icon into the "Applications" folder **(Figure 3.32)**. On macOS, the first time you open a new program, you will be prompted to confirm that you want to open the program since it was downloaded from the internet. Simply click "Open" to continue. In **Figure 3.33** you can see the default file Brackets opens up to and any promts asking for permission to share data with developers.

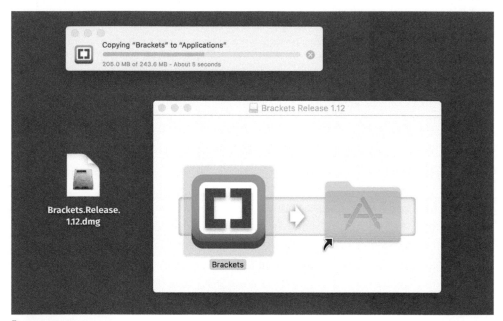

Figure 3.32

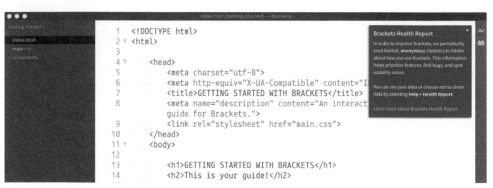

Figure 3.33

INSTALLING BROWSERSYNC

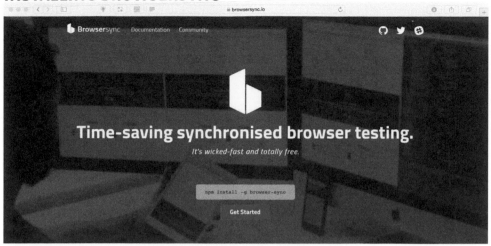

Figure 3.34

Installing Browsersync **(Figure 3.34)**, while simple, can be intimidating for graphic designers. It requires you to install multiple programs, and type commands in the command line via the macOS Terminal application. The first step is to go to https://www.browsersync.io/ and click on the "Get Started" button. This will take you to a set of instructions to follow **(Figure 3.35)**. However, following the "installers for macOS, Windows, and Linux" link will take you to a page with links to the actual programs. If you were a developer, you'd know what to do with these links.

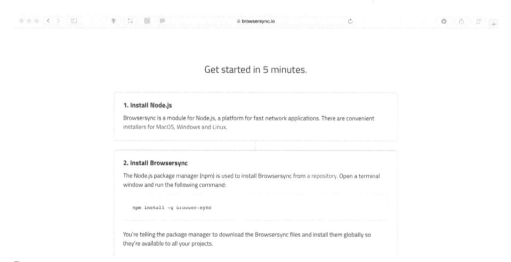

Figure 3.35

Since graphic designers are not developers—though they can be—it's best to go to https://nodejs.org/en/ to find the installer you need for your operating system. The website can detect what operating system you are using, so most likely you will see two buttons, one for an "LTS" version and the other for the "Current" version **(Figure 3.36)**. LTS stands for Long Term Support and represents the stable version of a program. The Current version is what is actively being developed and may contain bugs. For the purpose of this book, it's best to download the LTS version. At the time of this writing, the LTS version is 6.11.4, however, that version may change by the time you read this book, so simply look for the LTS version.

Figure 3.36

If the website doesn't detect your operating system, you will need to click on the "Downloads" link **(Figure 3.37)**. On this page you will find links to download the version that matches your operating system. Make sure to download the Installer, not the Binary. The Binary is the actual program, the Installer version is basically the Binary with an Installer bundled together.

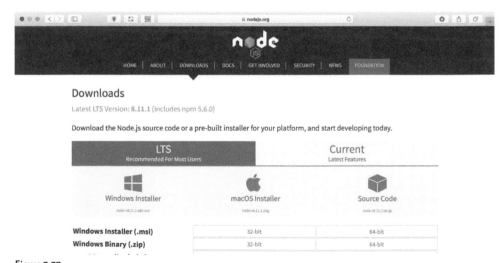

Figure 3.37

For macOS users, once the download is finished, double click the .pkg file to begin the installation process **(Figure 3.38)**.

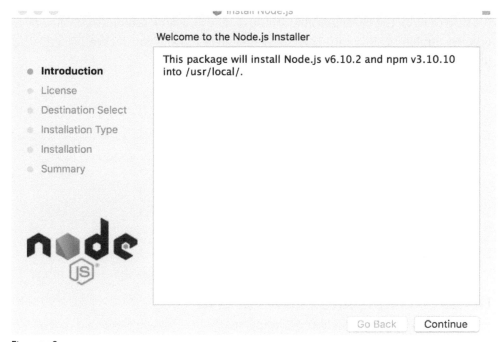

Figure 3.38

You will be prompted to agree to the license agreement. Once you've reviewed it, click "Agree" to continue. As Node.js is being installed, you may be prompted to enter your password to continue installation. Once you've entered your password, the installation process will begin. Once Node.js is installed, you can install Browsersync. At this time, you can also follow along with the directions on the Browsersync website for further details, or simply follow along with the instructions listed here.

The next step, if you are on a macOS system, is to open the program Terminal that is located in the Utilities folder. Once a Terminal window is open, simply type `npm install -g browser-sync` and hit the "Return" key to begin the installation process **(Figure 3.39)**.

2. Install Browsersync

The Node.js package manager (npm) is used to install Browsersync from a repository. Open a terminal window and run the following command:

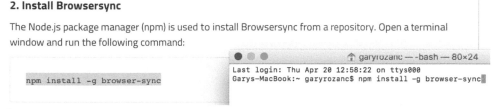

Figure 3.39

You will see a bunch of text scroll through the open Terminal window. Just ignore it, but don't close the open window until the text stops scrolling **(Figure 3.40)**.

It's safe to close the open Terminal window once you get a prompt that will let you type text again. At this point Browsersync is installed and you are ready to start using it.

Figure 3.40

USING BRACKETS AND BROWSER SYNC

Once you have both Brackets and Browsersync installed, you can begin to use the programs. It may seem a bit daunting at first, but after you do it once, it's actually pretty simple. To test this Native Application based workflow setup, you will need to download the exercise files at http://browsersdevicesfonts.com/exercise-files/03-getting-started.zip to begin. Once you have downloaded and unzipped the files, open up Brackets and click on the "Getting Started" drop down menu. Once you click on that, a dialogue box will pop up and then you need to click on the "Open Folder" option **(Figure 3.41)**. Navigate to the "03-getting-started" folder and click "Open" once you have it selected.

Once you have selected the folder, the "Getting Started" text will be replaced by the folder name, in this case "03-getting-started". You will also see the folder's contents listed as well **(Figure 3.42)**. To open any of the listed files double click on the file name, and the file will open so you can make edits. You will also see that any files that are currently open will appear in a newly created "Working Files" section above the "03-getting-started" folder contents.

Now that you have opened the files, you will be able to edit them the same way you edit files inside of CodePen's HTML and CSS panel editors. Open up the index.html file by double clicking on it. Once it's open, change `<p>Getting Start-ed with</p>` to `<p>Changing a Background Color</p>` **(Figure 3.43)**.

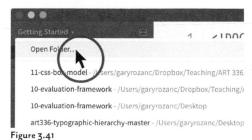

Figure 3.41

Figure 3.42

Once you make the change be sure to save the file, or you won't be able to see the updates you made.

```
14
15 ▼  <body>
16
17 ▼    <div>
18        <p>Changing Background Color</p>
19        <h1>Browsers, Devices, & Fonts</h
20      </div>
21
22
23
24    </body>
25
```

Figure 3.43

Next, try updating the CSS by clicking on the icon next to the CSS folder to expand the folder and reveal the style. css file. Replace #262626 with rebeccapurple (Figure 3.44). Once you start to type you will notice the Brackets will start to auto complete certain bits of code. Once the autocomplete dialogue box pops up, just click on what you want completed. This is a really nice feature that isn't currently available in CodePen.

```
3 ▼  body, html {
4       background-color: rebe
5       color: #fff;              rebeccapurple
6       display: grid;            darkslateblue
7       font-family: 'Scope Or    cornflowerblue
8       font-size: 22px;
9       height: 100%;
10   }
```

Figure 3.44

Now that you have changed the background color from dark gray/black to purple try adding a background image bay adding the following CSS. Note, Brackets will also try to autocomplete the image for you once you start typing. It may take a little time to get used to the timing on when to click, how much you actually need to type to start autocompleting, etc., so don't get frustrated (Figure 3.45)!

Your new CSS declaration should look like the following once you are done typing.

```
body {
    background image: url(../img/ghost-signs-low-rez.jpg);
    background-size: cover;
}
```

```
round-image: url(../img/)
                ../img/ghost-signs-low-rez.jpg

 auto;
ign: center;
```

Figure 3.45

To view your files on other devices that are connected to the same Wi-Fi network as your laptop or desktop computer you need to start up Browsersync. To do this on macOS open up the Terminal program and type cd followed by pressing the "Spacebar". Then drag the folder containing the files you want to view on different devices in the open Terminal window and press the "Return" key **(Figure 3.46)**. This will change the working directory from the root user folder to the "03-getting-started" folder **(Figure 3.47)**.

Figure 3.46

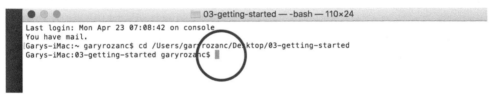

Figure 3.47

The next step is to start Browsersync and have it act as a web server. To do this, simply type browser-sync start --server --files '*.*' into the terminal window (command line) and press "Return" **(Figure 3.48)**.

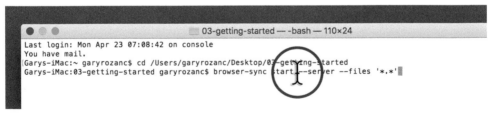

Figure 3.48

This will open the index.html page located inside the "03-getting-started" folder into your default browser using the "http://localhost:3000" URL. This URL will only work in the browser you have installed Browsersync on. To view the page across

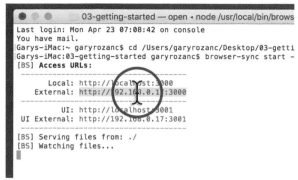

Figure 3.49

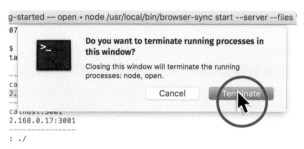

Figure 3.50

Figure 3.51

multiple devices connected to the same Wi-Fi network, copy and paste the external URL that I've highlighted. Your URL will most likely be different from the one in the example **(Figure 3.49)**, and that's OK. Just copy and paste it into a new tab in your browser.

As you are working, if you don't see the changes you are making appear in the browser, simply use the browser's refresh button to reload the page and you will be able to see your updated code changes. To close Browsersync, simply close out the Terminal app. When you do that, you will see a message asking you if you want to terminate the process that is running. Simply click the "Terminate" button and Browsersync will be disconnected **(Figures 3.50 & 3.51)**.

Final Thoughts on Workflow

When choosing the working method that is best for you, there are several things to consider such as cost, learning curve, features, etc. However, what really should be driving your decision is speed. The evaluations and tests that I will be covering in this book are necessary but do take time away from what you do best, *visual design*. Whichever method—Browser or Native Application based—is quicker for you to execute comfortably should be the leading factor in your final choice.

Using Your Device Lab

Using your device lab is fairly straightforward since your only goal is to get the contents of what you are viewing on your main workstation's browser into a browser on another device. The quickest way to do this is to take advantage of QR codes. Whether you are using the Browser or Native Application based workflow, the pages you are working on will have a fairly nebulous URL such as https://code-pen.io/browsersdevicesfonts/pen/yjYJvX or http://192.168.0.17:5757/ that you will need to enter into the browser on the device you want to evaluate and test on. Using one of the QR Code generator plugins on your main workstation's browser will give you a code **(Figure 3.52)** that you can scan with a QR reader app on the device you want to test it on.

Figure 3.52

This will save you the hassle of trying to type out those long URLs. If you are using the Native Application Based workflow, your workstation and mobile device must be connected to the same Wi-Fi network. If they aren't on the same network, the mobile device will not be able to connect, and you will get a blank screen or an error page depending on which browser you are using **(Figure 3.53)**.

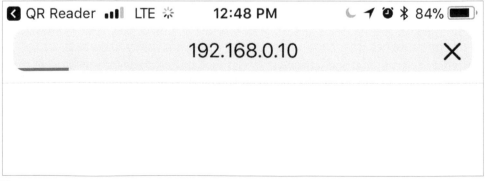

Figure 3.53

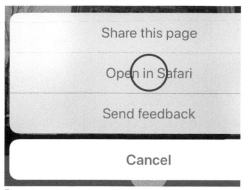

Figure 3.54

Now that you have generated a QR Code, simply use a QR Code reader on the device you want to test on to open up the URL, then open up the page in an actual browser **(Figure 3.54)**. Simply doing your evaluations and testing inside the QR Code reader won't reflect how users will actually be viewing your final design, which is through a standards compliant web browser, so don't skip this important step!

Using the Performance Test Server

It would be really nice if you could simply load your CodePens into one of the many website performance tests that exist. However, because CodePen is so easy to use there is a lot of performance killing code loaded into the page you don't see that will slow down the site and mask your visual design choices true performance. Also, if you are using the Native Application based workflow, your files are on your computer, not being delivered via a web server, so they don't have a way of being measured for performance either. To overcome these issues, you are going to upload your files to a web server that will temporarily host your files for testing and evaluating for performance.

Using the tool that I created for my own students you will get two unique URLs once your files are finished uploading. One URL will start with HTTP, the other with HTTPS. Since there are now two http protocols, HTTP and HTTP/2 you want to test for performance on both. How things are rendered in the browser can be drastically different between the two protocols and it's good to check your files in both environments. How you evaluate for performance will be covered in Chapter 04 *Typography* and Chapter 05 *Finding Breakpoints for Text & Images*. For now, I'm just going to demonstrate how to run the test.

01. If you are working in CodePen all you need to do is download the source files to your computer and unzip the folder.

02. If you are using the Native Application workflow you will need access to the folder where your working files are stored.

03. To get the URLs, drag and drop the folder with its contents into the browser window at https:// browsersdevicesfonts.com/performance and copy the two temporary URLs **(Figures 3.55 & 3.56)**.

Figure 3.55

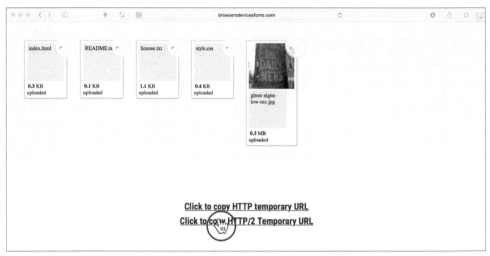

Figure 3.56

The files and URLs will be deleted from the server after 60 minutes. If you don't finish your tests within the allotted amount of time simply upload your files and start the tests again. It is also important to note that you must drag and drop the folder with the subfolders still intact. The tool is meant to upload the files exactly as they are structured when downloaded from CodePen or the book's companion website. Not dragging and dropping the folder as is (after you've made your updates to the HTML and CSS) will cause you to get an error or a file structure that isn't viewable by a web browser.

Webpage Test

Use the links generated from the performance testing server at Webpage Test: https://www.webpagetest.org/ and run your tests with the following "Advanced Settings" selected. The first time you visit Webpage Test you will need to click on the arrow next to "Advanced Settings" to expand the menu. Once you have pasted in one of the URLs click on the "Start Test" button and get in line for testing. Webpage Test is a popular service and may take a few minutes to run. Just leave your browser window open and come back and check on it a few minutes later. To test the second URL, open another browsers window and go back to WebPage test and paste in the URL and run a new test.

Figure 3.57

Figure 3.58

Again, I will cover what to evaluate for in the upcoming chapters. For now, you are running this test to get used to the tool and the process. However, I want to mention don't get fooled by the "Load Time". This isn't an accurate depiction of performance as experienced by a website's visitors. In an oversimplification, the "Load Time" is how long it takes for everything to be downloaded. The real metric you want to look at is in the "Filmstrip View". Once you click on the Filmstrip View link you will go to a page that gives you a visual timeline of what your website will look like in 10ths of a second. As you can see in my example, the user will see a blank white screen for .5 seconds. At .6 seconds they will see the background color, and by .7 seconds visitors will see an image start to appear.

Figure 3.59

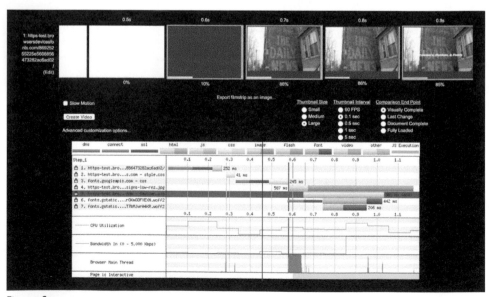

Figure 3.60

Final Thoughts

Just as there is no perfect workflow, there is no perfect device lab. Save yourself the headache and don't try to find the perfect solution for anything in the interactive design process; just design stuff. You will find that there are many more ways to achieve the same goals I set forth for you in this book with similar tools and processes. However, you are the lucky beneficiary of several years of my students going through this process with me in various forms until it was refined to its two simplest methods. Remember your main goal is to find a way to easily evaluate and test your designs in the same context that represents your potential users as quickly as possible, so you get to spend more time doing what you do best, design.

4 Typography

As discussed in Chapter 03 *Setting Up Your Toolbox* there are two distinct workflows for testing your designs in a browser across multiple devices. One method requires you to use Browser based applications for loading and viewing your typographic choices; the other method requires you to install native applications on your computer. It's up to you to decide the workflow you want to use; there isn't one single perfect working method.

How to utilize both of the workflows in your design process will be discussed in this chapter along with the pros and cons of each specific to typography. You will need the following regardless of which testing workflow you plan on using.

- Multiple devices to test on, a.k.a. your device lab.

- A free Typekit account: https://typekit.com/ if not already an Adobe CC subscriber.

- This link handy for quick access to Google Fonts: https://fonts.google.com/

- This link handy for quick access to open source fonts you can practice loading with the CSS property `@font-face` https://www. theleagueofmoveabletype.com/. Testing with `@font-face` only works with the paid subscription to CodePen Pro or the Native Application based workflow.

What You Will Need for a Browser Based Workflow

This is the quickest option because you don't have to install anything. This work-flow lets you quickly share your typographic choices in code with a front-end developer, and you have access to a free device emulator necessary to determine proper font weights if you don't have a robust device lab. However, it doesn't let you test fonts loaded via the CSS property `@font-face` without a paid subscription to CodePen Pro and this is an important distinction. In this instance I would recommend a CodePen Pro subscription because it lets you test fonts using `@font-face` and since the device emulator is already free for CodePen users this becomes an all-in-one workflow. At the time of this writing CodePen Pro will cost you $12.00 a month or $108.00 a year.

Now back to actual evaluating and testing. While you choose your fonts, the front-end developer will most likely decide the best method for implementing them on the final website. If supplying the fonts from Google Fonts or Typekit are not an option—because of availability or performance—the fonts may have to be self-hosted and if you don't do any evaluations or tests with them you could end up having to resolve those issues during front-end development or worse, once the site is live and that will cost time and money to fix. For the Browser based workflow you will need the following.

- A free CodePen http://codepen.io/ account

- A free CrossBrowserTesting https://crossbrowsertesting.com/freetrial trial account.

- Optional, but recommended: upgrade to a CodePen Pro account to be able to evaluate and test fonts using the CSS property @font-face. You will also utilize the Pro account for testing and evaluating images later in this book if that helps you decided. However, you can do this evaluation and testing with the Native Application based workflow without the need for CodePen or a CodePen Pro account.

What You Will Need for a Native Application Based Workflow

This method requires a bit more time to set up and requires you to learn a little bit more HTML and CSS since CodePen won't be handling some behind the scenes writing and linking of HTML and CSS files. However, you will be able to evaluate, and test fonts loaded via @font-face, and images discussed in a later chapter for without any paid subscriptions. Another bonus with this workflow is you are in control of your own work since the applications and files live on your computer, not in the cloud. The only negative to this method is not being able to have access to the device emulator that's free for CodePen users for evaluating fonts in browsers and operating systems you physically don't have access to which will be discussed later in the chapter. It will cost you around $150.00 a year, or $19.99 a month to get access to a device emulator such as BrowserStack.

- Brackets http://brackets.io/ already installed.

- Browsersync https://www.browsersync.io/ already installed.

- QR code reader and writer applications already installed.

What You Will Need for Performance Testing

How fast a website loads is a critical issue that most graphic designers overlook. If a viewer doesn't perceive that the website is going to deliver what they want within one second, and is not fully loaded within two seconds, or three seconds on a mobile device, they will abandon the page.[1,2] Most of the poor performance issues out there are because of visual design choices, not internet connectivity or web server issues. To test to see if your design choices are going to slow down the delivery of a website to a crawl, you'll need to upload your files to a web server. Keep the https:// browsersdevicesfonts.com/performance/ link handy for quick access for HTTP and HTTP2 performance testing.

---

1   Sutter, Brian. 2017. Vrooom! Why Website Speed Matters. https://www.entrepreneur.com/article/281986 (accessed April 27, 2018).

2   Everts, Tammy. 2016. Google: 53% of mobile users abandon sites that take longer than 3 seconds to load. https://www.soasta.com/blog/google-mobile-web-performance-study/ (accessed April 22, 2018).

*Part One: Creating HTML &
CSS Pages for Context*

Before we get into the exact details of what you need to look for in your visual designs to ensure that it meets the needs of your end user regardless of device, and why you need to test your typographic choices in the browser, you need something to actually test. The two HTML pages you will need to work with are available to be forked at CodePen and are available to be downloaded from this book's companion website if you're working with the Native Application based workflow.

The purpose behind these two pages is to give you the necessary context to identify the common typographic issues users will face once your site goes live. To get the maximum benefit of this process it's best that you follow the steps below creating the necessary testing and evaluation pages first. You may be tempted to skip ahead to the section that you feel is most relevant to you. However, since each demonstration in each chapter builds off the previous one, skipping ahead will make it difficult to complete future demonstrations. Upon finishing this book, you will be able to incorporate the evaluations and tests as best fits your own workflow. Once you have the two pages created, I will go in depth on what you need to evaluate and test them for.

Font Specimen Page

Each browser and operating system renders fonts differently. Some fonts you can hardly notice the difference, others can be quite drastic. For example, a regular weight font could look almost bolded in some browsers and operating systems and you'd be better off using the light version depending on what best suits your end user. You also have to plan on the fact that different devices have different screen resolutions and pixel densities and are read at varying distances than the device you are creating your mockups on. So, what you are thinking is easy to read at about a foot and a half away while comfortably seated in front of your 27" retina display will not be as easy to read on a smartphone at arm's length. To ensure that your font choices are going to be easily readable simply looking at your font of choice across a few different devices and browsers at a few different sizes will give you a strong indication of what your fonts will look like in real time, ensure that they work across all viewing environments as intended, and give you the accurate information to work with in your layout program and pass along to your front-end developer. How to evaluate and test these choices will be covered in Part 2 of this chapter.

There are many different options for delivering non-system fonts to your user's browser. I'm not going to discuss the merits of which delivery method to use in this book, that's a conversation you have with your front-end developer. Instead, I'm going to show you three different methods for delivering web fonts that should cover most options you'll experience in the wild.

For this demo, you will be working either directly in CodePen or using Brackets and Browsersync. However, before you start coding, you will need to make font choices. To save pages in this book and keep things from getting too repetitive between the two different workflows I will discuss the font selection process then divide that into a Browser and Native Application subsection. This will allow each reader to do the common tasks for each workflow first then "Choose Your Own" workflow. When it's appropriate to skip ahead based on workflow method I will let you know.

Google Fonts

Google Fonts free service is easy to use and integrates with many Content Management Systems (CMS) such as Squarespace and WordPress. Google's servers and global content delivery network should provide adequate performance for most users. Finally, it may be the best choice for your use case, so it's good to know how to use them.

To get started head to the Google Fonts website at https://fonts.google.com/. You can pick whatever font you want to use for this demo, but I'm going to use "Passion One" because it has multiple styles and is different enough from default fonts that you will know it's been loaded by the web browser. You can use the Google Fonts search feature or simply follow this URL https://fonts.google.com/specimen/Passion+One to go directly to the Passion One specimen page.

Click on the "Select This Font" button. You can also click on the red "+" button to select a font for use from the main page **(Figure 4.1)**. You are not limited to selecting one font, but for now only pick one. Once you select the font, you will see a dialogue box at the bottom of the screen labeled "1 Family Selected". Click on the dialogue box to expand it and reveal options to embed fonts on your website and select different weights and language sets when available.

With the dialogue box open select the "Customize" tab to bring up the different weight options **(Figure 4.2)**. For now, just select one weight. I picked Passion One bold 700. Finally, click on the "Embed" tab and copy the text that starts with "@" that is in between the `<style></style>` tags **(Figure 4.3)**. You will need to paste `@import url('https://fonts.googleapis.com/css?family=Passion+One:700');` and the `font-family: 'Passion One', cursive;` (or the CSS for the font you picked) into CodePen or Brackets so keep this text or open dialogue box handy. The rest

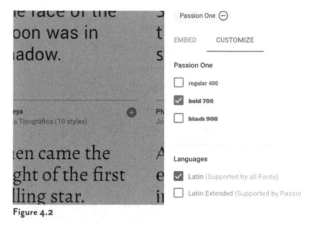

Figure 4.1

Figure 4.2

of the steps will need to be completed in either the Browser or Native Application based workflow. Since this is the first time you will really work in either, I suggest trying both workflows for this demo for a better sense of which you may prefer.

Figure 4.3

Browser Based Workflow

If you have already decided to use the Native Application based workflow you can skip ahead to that section.

1. Fork the Font Specimen Evaluation Page pen at https://codepen.io/browsersdevicesfonts/pen/erZbMM and leave it open in your browser.

2. Paste the text `@import url('https://fonts.googleapis.com/css?family=Passion+One:700');` CSS from Google Fonts into your newly forked pen's CSS section.

3. In the CSS panel type `body {}`, then paste the text `font-family: font-family: 'Passion One', cursive;` or whatever font you picked in between the `{}` so yours looks like

```
body {
   font-family: 'Passion One', cursive;
}
```

4. Yours should look similar to mine when you are done, and you should see the fonts change from either a system font such as Arial or Times to Passion One or the font you selected **(Figure 4.4)**.

Figure 4.4

5. Click on the "Actions" or "Change View" button and then click on the "Full Page" button to see what your font choice looks like without the extra HTML, CSS, and JS sections open.

If you have already decided to use the Browser based workflow you can skip ahead to the *Using Typekit Hosted Fonts on Your Font Specimen Page* section.

1 Download and unzip the 04-01-font-specimen-page.zip file from the book's website at http://browsersdevicesfonts.com/exercise-files/04-01-font-specimen-evaluation-page.zip

2 Rename the folder to "font-specimen-google-fonts" and open the newly created folder using Brackets by clicking on the "Getting Started" dropdown menu if this is your first time using Brackets. Brackets remembers the folder you most recently worked in, so you may not see a folder titled "Getting Started". No matter the tittle, the working folder will always be in the same location and selectable, so you can change it. Review Chapter 03 *Setting Up Your Toolbox* for a refresher on using Brackets.

3 Open the style.css file located in the CSS folder and paste in the following code `@import url('https://fonts.googleapis.com/css?family=Passion+One:700');` copied from Google Fonts.

4 Continue working in the style.css file and type in `body {}`, then paste the text `font-family: font-family: 'Passion One', cursive;` **(Figure 4.3)** or the font you picked in between the {} so yours looks like

```
body {
    font-family: 'Passion One', cursive;
}
```

5 Yours should look similar to mine when you are done, and you should see the fonts change from a system font such as Arial or Times to Passion One or the font you selected **(Figure 4.5)**.

Figure 4.5

6 To immediately check if the font loaded, click on "Live Preview" to open the index.html file in Chrome. If the font did not change, make sure you saved the changes to the index.html and style.css files **(Figure 4.6)**.

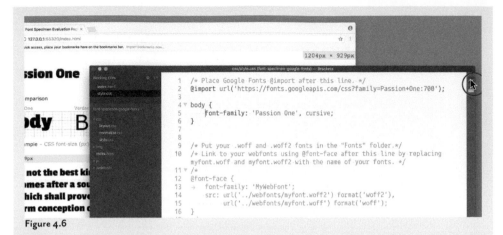

Figure 4.6

 In the index.html file there isn't much you need to change. Just update the font name for clarity when handing off the files to your front-end developer **(Figure 4.7)**.

Figure 4.7

In order for you to evaluate your choices on other devices which is discussed later in this chapter, you will need to reference how to start Browsersync in Chapter 03 *Setting Up Your Toolbox* for the Native Application workflow. Both the Browser and Native Application use the QR code generator method to create a QR code linking to the pen. You can reference that method in Chapter 03 as well.

Typekit

Most graphic designers already have an Adobe Creative Cloud subscription which comes with use of Typekit, but if you or your client don't have a subscription, it's one of the more robust, yet inexpensive web font services out there. Finally, and most importantly for this demo, Typekit has an authorization process so others can't use your kit. To secure your kit from pirated use on other sites, Typekit asks you to enter the domain name of the site that will be using the kit. Many other subscription type services do this as well, so knowing how to use Typekit should give you insights on how to use the other web font hosting services.

No matter the workflow method you have decided upon, go to Typekit https://typekit.com, login and look for the "<> Kits" button and hover over it to open the dropdown menu and then click on the "+ Create new Kit" button **(Figure 4.8)**.

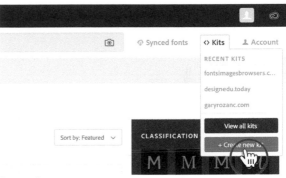

Figure 4.8

In the new dialogue window that opens up give a name to the kit that you will remember; I'm going to use "Font Specimen - Eldwin Script". In the "Domains" section, type in the following

- For CodePen add: **s.codepen.io**

- For Brackets Live Preview: **127.0.0.1**

- For Browsersync you will need to reference Chapter 03 on how to get the external URL if you don't remember **(Figures 4.9 & 4.10)**. Typing my Browsersync generated URL will not work for you!

In my kit I entered all three URLs separated by a comma: **s.codepen.io, 127.0.0.1, 192.168.0.17**. If you don't enter the URL, Typekit won't authorize CodePen, Bracket's Live Preview, or Browsersync to use the font you selected **(Figure 4.11)**.

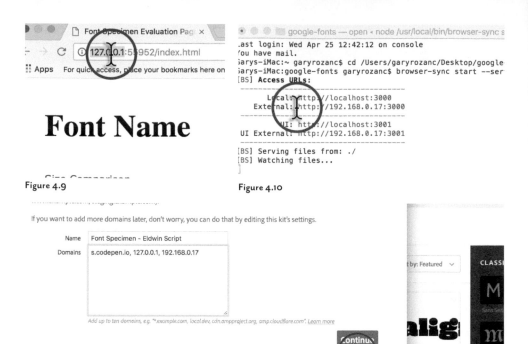

Figure 4.9

Figure 4.10

Figure 4.11

Next, click "Continue". In the new window click on the "@import" tab and copy the line of code between the `<style></style>` tags **(Figure 4.12)**. Set aside this line of code to paste into CodePen or Brackets later in this demo.

Figure 4.12

Figure 4.13

Click "Continue" and then click "Browse All Fonts" to begin to select a font to evaluate. This won't open up the fonts in the new window; rather you will need to go back to the original window. Click on a font to open its specimen page. For this demo, I'm using Eldwin Script, https://ty-pekit.com/fonts/eldwin-script but you can pick your own. Next, click on the "<> ADD TO KIT" button to add the font to the newly created kit **(Figures 4.13 & 4.14)**.

You will be redirected back to the mini-window. Here you will be able to choose font-weights to test. Since this isn't

Figure 4.14

a performance test, just leave them all checked. Next, click "Publish" **(Figure 4.15)**. If you forget to click publish your kit won't be available and you won't see the new font displayed in your evaluation page.

Figure 4.15

Finally, click on the "Using weights & styles in your CSS" link. Copy the family name, style, and weight **(Figure 4.16)** so you can paste that information into your CodePen or style.css file via Brackets.

Using weights & styles in your CSS

To access specific weights & styles, or *variations*, of this font in your CSS, use these values for font-family, font-weight, and font-style:

Variation	font-family	font-weight	font-style	Copy CSS
Thin	"eldwin-script"	200	normal	
Light	"eldwin-script"	300	normal	
Regular	"eldwin-script"	400	normal	
SemiBold	"eldwin-script"	600	normal	
Bold	"eldwin-script"	700	normal	
Heavy	"eldwin-script"	900	normal	

☐ Show variation-specific font-family names. When are these necessary?

Figure 4.16

Browser Based Workflow

If you have already decided to use the Native Application based workflow you can skip ahead to that section.

① Fork the Font Specimen Evaluation Page pen at https://codepen.io/browsersdevicesfonts/pen/erZbMM and leave it open in your browser.

② Paste the embed code you copied from Typekit into your newly forked pen's CSS section. `@import url("https://use.typekit.net/kah2hcd.css");` Yours will not be the same as mine but will look very similar.

③ In the CSS panel type `body {}`, then paste the text you copied from Typekit. If you also picked Eldwin Script the CSS will look like the following **(Figure 4.17)**.

```
body {
    font-family: eldwin-script;
    font-style: normal;
    font-weight: 200;
}
```

Figure 4.17

Yours should look similar to mine when you are done, and you should see the fonts change from a system font such as Arial or Times to Eldwin Script or the font you selected. Click on the "Actions" or "Change View" button and then click on the "Full Page" button to see what your font choice looks like without the extra HTML, CSS, and JS sections open.

Native Application Based Workflow

If you have already decided to use the Browser based workflow you can skip ahead to the *Using Self-hosted Fonts on Your Font Specimen Page via CSS's* `@font-face` *property* section.

1 Download and unzip the 04-01-font-specimen-page.zip file from the book's website at http://browsersdevicesfonts.com/exercise-files/04-01-font-specimen-evaluation-page.zip

2 Rename the folder to "font-specimen-typekit" and open the newly created folder using Brackets by clicking on the "Getting Started" dropdown menu if this is your first time using Brackets. Brackets remembers the folder you most recently worked in, so you may not see a folder titled "Getting Started".

3 Open the style.css file located in the CSS folder and paste the embed code you copied from Typekit. `@import url("https://use.typekit.net/kah2hcd.css");` Yours will not be the same, but will look similar.

4 Continuing work in the style.css file and type in the following `body {}`, then paste the text you copied from Typekit. If you also picked Eldwin Script the CSS will look like the following **(Figure 4.18)**.

```
body {
    font-family: eldwin-script;
    font-style: normal;
    font-weight: 200;
}
```

Figure 4.18

5 To immediately check if the font loaded, click on "Live Preview" to open the index.html file in Chrome **(Figure 4.19)**. If the font did not change, make sure you saved the changes to the index.html and style.css files. Yours should look similar to mine when you are done, and you should see the fonts change from either a system font such as Arial or Times to Eldwin Script or the font you selected.

6 In the index.html file there isn't much you need to change. Just update the font name for clarity when handing the files over to your front-end developer.

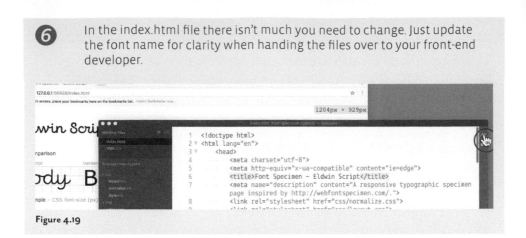

Figure 4.19

Self-hosted Fonts

Quite literally, there are times when self-hosting may be your only option if the font you choose isn't available through one of the commercially hosted web font services. Plus, if you were to break down how both Google Fonts and Typekit technically load fonts into your browser, they are doing it with the same `@font-face` property I'm going to cover in this demonstration. They just have you link to their CSS instructions instead of loading the font through your own style sheet. So, it's good to know how fonts are actually loaded by the browser.

To get started using either workflow method, you will need your own web fonts to self-host that you will upload to the Asset Manager in CodePen Pro or use from your computer for the Native Application based workflow. There are two ways to get web fonts, find an existing web font or convert a TTF or OTF you already have that is licensed for web use by converting it with a Web Font Generator.[3] It's important to note that not all fonts are authorized for conversion using Web Font Generator, so read your license carefully. For this demonstration you are going to download the popular open source font League Gothic from The League of Moveable Type https://www.theleagueofmoveabletype.com/league-gothic.

Once you have downloaded the file, unzip it and locate the "webfonts" folder and look for the font ending in ".woff" or ".woff2" if that's the only one available. For this demo I'm going to use League Gothic Condensed Regular, leaguegothic-condensed-regular-webfont.woff.

---

3   Dunham, Ethan. 2018. Font Squirrel Webfont Generator. https://www.fontsquirrel.com/tools/webfont-generator/ (accessed April 27, 2018).

If you have already decided to use the Native Application based workflow you can skip ahead to that section. If you want to stick with the Browser based workflow, you will need to upgrade to CodePen Pro to be able to use the asset hosting feature. If you don't want to upgrade, you can evaluate and test self-hosted fonts using the Native Application based workflow demonstrated in the next section.

 Fork the Font Specimen Evaluation Page pen at https://codepen.io/browsersdevicesfonts/pen/erZbMM and type the following into the CSS panel **(Figure 4.20)**.

```css
@font-face {
    font-family: " ";
    src: url(' ') format('woff');
    font-weight: ;
    font-style: ;
}

body {
    font-family: " ";
}
```

Figure 4.20

 Upload your .woff file to CodePen using the Asset Manager by clicking on the "Assets" button on the bottom of the forked pen screen and then click on the "Choose Files" button and look for the "leaguegothic-condensed-regular-webfont.woff" file and then click "choose" to upload the font. Copy the URL and close out the Asset Manager panel **(Figure 4.21)**. You will only have access to the Asset Management feature with a Pro subscription.

Figure 4.21

③ Back in your pen's CSS panel update your CSS to look like the following. Replace the URL in the code below with the one you just copied. You will also need to use a different name for the font-family if using a different font. However, the name you give to font-family is arbitrary. I could have used League Gothic, league-gothic-condensed, etc., as long as I use the same name consistently throughout my CSS when I want to display the content using the custom font. Replace . . . with the URL supplied by the CodePen Asset Manager **(Figure 4.22)**.

```
@font-face {
    font-family: "League Gothic Condensed";
    src: url('https://.../leaguegothic-con-
densed-regular-webfont.woff') format('woff');
    font-weight: normal;
    font-style: normal;
}

body {
    font-family: "League Gothic Condensed";
}
```

Figure 4.22

Once you are done typing and uploading the font files you should see the new font loaded into the specimen page. If the font did not change, make sure you saved the pen. If that doesn't work, you may need to refresh the page.

Native Application Based Workflow

You will need to read the Using *Brackets and Browsersync* section in Chapter 03 if this your first time using the Native Application workflow. If you have already decided to use the Browser based workflow by upgrading to a CodePen Pro subscription you can skip ahead to the *Creating a Typographic Hierarchy Page for Evaluation* section.

① Download and unzip the 04-01-font-specimen-page.zip file from the book's website at http://browsersdevicesfonts.com/exercise-files/04-01-font-specimen-evaluation-page.zip

② Rename the folder to "font-specimen-page-@font-face" and open the newly created folder using Brackets by clicking on the "Getting Started" dropdown menu if this is your first time using Brackets. Brackets remembers the folder you most recently worked in, so you may not see a folder titled "Getting Started".

③ Open the style.css file located in the CSS folder and use the Brackets text editor to type the following into the styles.css file.

```css
@font-face {
    font-family: " ";
    src: url(' ') format('woff');
    font-weight: ;
    font-style: ;
}

body {
    font-family: " ";
}
```

④ Next, you need to copy the leaguegothic-condensed-regular-webfont.woff file to the "webfonts" folder **(Figure 4.23)**.

► ▓ css		Today at 10:18 PM
► ▓ img		Jan 28, 2018 at 8:41 PM
☉ index.html		Apr 24, 2018 at 8:43 PM
► ▓ js		Today at 10:18 PM
▼ ▓ webfonts		Today at 10:19 PM
▓ leaguegothic-cond...gular-webfont.woff		Mar 19, 2014 at 9:38 AM

x
Drive
ɔ
Ɔrive
ents
ads

Figure 4.23

⑤ Back in the style.css file update your code to look like the following. Note, the name you give to font-family is arbitrary. I could have used League Gothic, league-gothic-condensed, etc., as long as I use the same name consistently throughout my CSS when I want to display the content using the custom font **(Figure 4.24)**.

```css
@font-face {
    font-family: "League Gothic Condensed";
    src: url('../webfonts/leaguegothic-con-
densed-regular-webfont.woff') format('woff')
    font-weight: normal;
    font-style: normal;
}

body {
    font-family: "League Gothic Condensed";
}
```

Figure 4.24

To immediately check if the font loaded, click on "Live Preview" to open the index.html file in Chrome **(Figure 4.25)**. If the font did not change, make sure you saved the changes to the index.html and style.css files. In the index.html file there isn't much you

```
1   <!doctype html>
2 ▼ <html lang="en">
3 ▼   <head>
4       <meta charset="utf-8">
5       <meta http-equiv="x-ua-compatible" content="ie=edge">
6       <title>Font Specimen Evaluation Page</title>
7       <meta name="description" content="A responsive typographic specimen
        page inspired by http://webfontspecimen.com/.">
8       <link rel="stylesheet" href="css/normalize.css">
9       <link rel="stylesheet" href="css/layout.css">
10      <link rel="stylesheet" href="css/style.css">
11    </head>
12    <body>
13 ▼   <main role="main">
14        <h1>League Gothic Condensed<!-- Replace with your font name. --
          ></h1>
15
16 ▼     <section class="body-size">
17          <h2>Size Comparison</h2>
18 ▼        <div class="body-size-grid">
19            <h3>League Gothic Condensed<!-- Replace with your font
              name. -->
```

Figure 4.25

need to change. However, you may find it helpful to add the font name for clarity when handing the files over to your front-end developer.

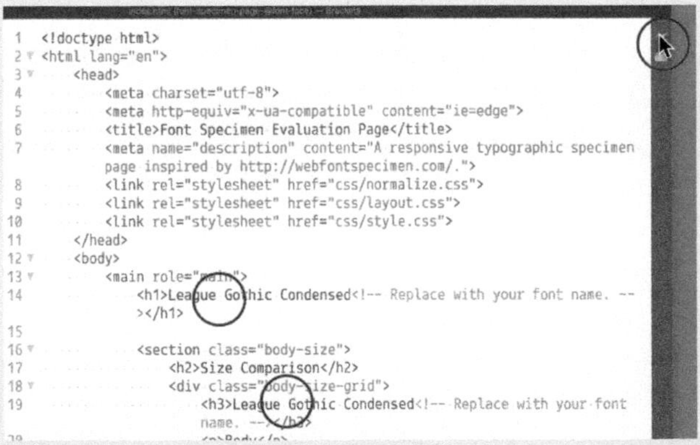

Typographic Hierarchy Page

While the font specimen page will go a long way in helping you identify the right size font for the main body copy or ideal headline size, it doesn't do much to help you figure out the typographic scale between headlines, sub-headlines, body copy, captions, and more. Nor does it help you determine if your font pairings look the same in your static mockup as they will on the responsive web.

Fortunately, the typographic hierarchy page you will be creating will let you see your choices in context. Seeing typographic hierarchy in context will let you know if you need more space between headlines and body copy, between sections of content, and more. Modifying this typographic hierarchy page will give you the necessary content and context to evaluate for scale, font pairing, and to check to ensure optimal performance, so users don't abandon the site because it took too long for the text to become viewable.

For this demo, you will be working either directly in CodePen or using Brackets and Browsersync. You can either follow along and make the same font choices that I'm using in the demonstrations, or you can make your own choices. Either way, to give you the most flexibility, I will be choosing a body font, with matching bold and italic font from Typekit. I will also be using one headline font and mono-spaced font from Google Fonts to demonstrate how easy it is to mix and match fonts from the different web font services.

Before you get started with whichever workflow method you prefer, it's good to take a look at the default typographic hierarchy that is applied when marking up the content with HTML **(Figure 4.26)**. While it's not in the scope of this book to discuss what a good typographic hierarchy looks like, it's important to note that the default hierarchy of many of the HTML elements can make it confusing for users to read your website's content. It's also important to note the performance of the page. As you can see in the WebPage Speed Test results, covered in depth in the upcoming *Evaluating and Testing* section, the webpage loads very quickly using default system fonts **(Figure 4.27)**. Poor typographic choices such as loading too many web fonts can adversely affect a site's performance, but more on that in the *Evaluating and Testing Your Choices* section.

1269px26   + Toggle 45-75 characters.

Introduction to web typography

Web typography refers to the use of fonts on the World Wide Web. When HTML was first created, font faces and styles were controlled exclusively by the settings of each Web browser. There was no mechanism for individual Web pages to control font display until Netscape introduced the <font> tag in 1995, which was then standardized in the HTML 2 specification. However, the font specified by the tag had to be installed on the user's computer or a fallback font, such as a browser's default sans-serif or monospace font, would be used. The first Cascading Style Sheets specification was published in 1996 and provided the same capabilities.

The **CSS2 specification** was released in 1998 and attempted to improve the font selection process by adding font matching, synthesis and download. These techniques did not gain much use, and were removed in the CSS2.1 specification. However, Internet Explorer added support for the font downloading feature in version 4.0, released in 1997.[1] Font downloading was later included in the **CSS3 fonts module**, and has since been implemented in Safari 3.1, Opera 10 and Mozilla Firefox 3.5. This has subsequently increased interest in Web typography, as well as the usage of font downloading.

CSS1

In the first CSS specification[2], authors specified font characteristics via a series of properties:

- font-family
- font-style
- font-variant
- font-weight
- font-size

All fonts were identified solely by name. Beyond the properties mentioned above, designers had no way to style fonts, and no mechanism existed to select fonts not present on the client system.

Web-safe fonts

Web-safe fonts are fonts likely to be present on a wide range of computer systems, and used by Web content authors to increase the likelihood that content displays in their chosen font. If a visitor to a Web site does not have the specified font, their browser tries to select a similar alternative, based on the author-specified fallback fonts and generic families or it uses font substitution defined in the visitor's operating system.

Figure 4.26

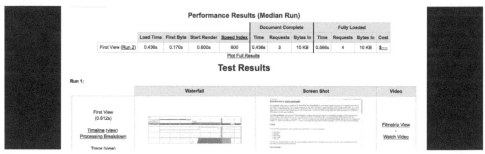

Figure 4.27

Browser Based Workflow

If you have already decided to use the Native Application based workflow you can skip ahead to that section.

1 Fork the Typographic Hierarchy Page - Template pen at https://codepen.io/browsersdevicesfonts/pen/YLpQZG and rename the newest pen to something that is descriptive of the evaluation purpose. For example, change the name to the client's name or website URL that you would be working on. For this demonstration I'm going to rename the pen to "Typographic Hierarchy Page - Demo."

2 Next, add a font for the body copy in the same way you did for the Font Specimen demo. For this demonstration, I'm going to use Calluna Sans from Exljbris Font Foundry in Light, Light Italic, and Semi Bold from Typekit. Don't forget to add the Embed Code if you are using TypeKit in the CSS editor panel. Yours will look like this if you are using Calluna.

```
| @import url("https://use.typekit.net/hup3cob.css");

| body {
|   font-family: "calluna-sans", sans-serif;
|   font-weight: 300;
|   font-style: normal;
| }
```

③ To ensure that the browser loads the italic and bold versions of the font, be sure to update the CSS with the following if you are using Calluna Sans, or the corresponding style and weight of the fonts you have chosen **(Figure 4.28)**.

```
| i, em {
|   font-style: italic;
| }

| b, strong {
|   font-weight: 600;
| }
```

Figure 4.28

Finally, you are going to load two additional fonts. The first I want you to add is a headline font that will be used to help distinguish between different sections within the page. Next, if you read through the article you will notice that it makes reference to CSS terms. There is an HTML element called <code> that lets users and search engines know that the text enclosed within the <code> element is a programming language. By default, the <code> element will display text in a monospace font similar to what you see in the CodePen editor.

For both the headline text and code text I'm going to use the Roboto family. Specifically Roboto Slab and Roboto Mono from Google Fonts by adding it the same way as demonstrated in the Font Specimen demo, but this time the @import will be loading two fonts, not one **(Figure 4.29)**.

```
@import url('https://fonts.googleapis.com/css?fami-
ly=Roboto+Mono:300|Roboto+Slab:700');

h1 {
  font-family: 'Roboto Slab', serif;
  font-weight: 700;
}


code {
  font-family: 'Roboto Mono', monospace;
  font-weight: 300;
}
```

Figure 4.29

When you are done updating your CSS you should see the font change in your browser. If you don't see the change, try closing the windows and emptying your browser's cache/history. Web browsers store certain files to make return visits to the site faster. This caching will sometimes stop you from seeing the multiple changes you made to your fonts.

Native Application Based Workflow

If you have already decided to use the Browser based workflow you can skip ahead to the What's Next? section.

1 To begin, download the Typographic Hierarchy Page Template at https://browsersdevicesfonts.com/exercise-files/04-02-typographic-hierarchy-page-template.zip and open the folder up in Brackets, and start Browsersync.

2 Next, add a font for the body copy in the same way you did for the Font Specimen demo. For this demo, I'm going to use Calluna Sans from Exljbris Font Foundry in Regular, Italic, and Bold from Typekit. Don't forget to add the Embed Code if you are using Typekit in the style.css file. Your CSS will look like this if you are using Calluna Sans, though your @ import will look a bit different.

```css
@import url("https://use.typekit.net/hup3cob.css");

body {
    font-family: "calluna-sans", sans-serif;
    font-weight: 300;
    font-style: normal;
}
```

3 To ensure that the browser loads the italic and bold versions of the font, be sure to update the CSS with the following if you are using Calluna Sans, or the corresponding style and weight of the fonts you have chosen.

```css
i, em {
    font-style: italic;
}

b, strong {
    font-weight: 600;
}
```

4 Finally, you are going to load two additional fonts. The first I want you to add is a headline font that will be used to help distinguish between different sections. Next, if you read through the article you will notice that it makes reference to CSS terms. There is an HTML element called

`<code>` that lets users and search engines know that the text enclosed within the `<code>` element is a programming language. By default, the `<code>` element will display text in a monospace font similar to what you see in the CodePen editor.

For both the headline text and code text I'm going to use the Roboto family. Specifically Roboto Slab and Roboto Mono from Google Fonts by adding it the same way as demonstrated in the Font Specimen demo, but this time the `@import` will be loading two fonts, not one.

```
@import url('https://fonts.googleapis.com/css?fami-
ly=Roboto+Mono:300|Roboto+Slab:700');

h1 {
    font-family: 'Roboto Slab', serif;
    font-weight: 700;
}

code {
    font-family: 'Roboto Mono', monospace;
    font-weight: 300;
}
```

To immediately check if the font loaded, click on "Live Preview" to open the index.html file in Chrome. If the font did not change, make sure you saved the changes to the index.html and style.css files. In the index.html file there isn't anything you need to change **(Figure 4.30)**.

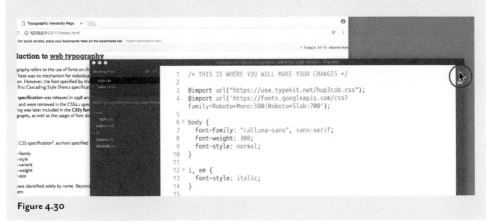

Figure 4.30

Finally, now that the Typographic Hierarchy Page has the fonts loaded that were just demonstrated, I've rerun the page through the Web Page Test to evaluate for performance. You will learn to do this later, but I want to show you the difference in average first view times between using default system fonts (.436 seconds) versus loading five unique web fonts (1.24 seconds) **(Figure 4.31)**.

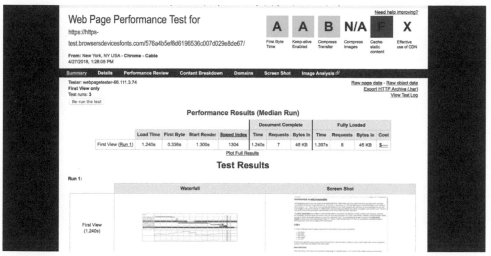

Figure 4.31

Now that you have learned how to make a font specimen page, you can make a new page for all your font choices prior to starting to design your visual mockups in a layout program. While you may not like digital clutter, I suggest saving each pen/page—hence the suggestion for proper naming conventions—you make so you can reference it later when you begin a new project. Saving these pages will also be discussed in the final chapter where you make style guides to hand off to your developer.

*Part Two: Evaluating &
Testing Your Choices*

Before reading any further, if you haven't completed the demos for both the *Font Specimen Page* and the *Typographic Hierarchy Page* do so now! It's much easier to do all the necessary evaluations and performance testing if you have both pages in front of you at once.

There are many thought pieces out there making the claim that the web is composed of 95% typography.[4,5] I'm not going to argue or defend the science or accuracy of these claims, but one thing is certain: Most people now get their information on screen-based devices, and it's the graphic designer's job to make sure all the content is presented in the most legible way possible. In my experience, graphic designers creating for a screen-based medium often overlook the legibility of typography not only for long-form reading, but for critical content like input forms necessary to collect credit card information, or captions to charts, photos, and tables. There is a lot of critical instruction that the user must be able to read to complete a given task. The key word in the last sentence is *user*, and every good designer knows that anything they create needs to work for the user if the design is going to be effective. However, designing for a user for any screen-based interaction, whether reading an article or filling out a form, is problematic at best and impossible to determine at worst.

To get a better sense of just how unpredictable the use cases of the end user can be, let's pretend we know who the user is. For this exercise, I created a persona for a digital subscriber to The New York Times. Her name is Kate. Prior to the smartphone and tablet revolution, Kate read the print edition of The New York Times held at a comfortable reading distance for her eyesight, mostly indoors where she had room to spread out and flip through all the pages of the newspaper without disturbing anyone around her. This use case meant ensuring pictures are big enough so details within the photo can easily be seen and making sure the type is easy for a person with average eyesight to read at about forearm's length from the body. Kate would then adjust the reading distance to suit the needs brought about by her immediate surroundings, time of day, and eyesight accordingly.

---

4 Reichenstein, Oliver. 2006. Web Design is 95% Typography. https://ia.net/topics/the-web-is-all-about-typography-period/ (accessed April 22, 2018).

5 Scrivens, Paul. 2012. One More Time: Typography is the Foundation of Web Design. https://www.smashingmagazine.com/2012/07/one-more-time-typography-is-the-foundation-of-web-design/ (accessed April 22, 2018).

To test the usability of the newspaper layout, a designer would print it on lower contrast paper, similar to newsprint, and hold it at forearm's length to see if it's legible. If the text is too small or too big, or if the images don't look right, you can quickly go into your layout program and make the necessary adjustments. This was an easy testing process that could be done within minutes. Now let's talk about how Kate reads the digital edition of The New York Times today. If she's at home, she will read on her tablet device; if she's out and about waiting for the bus or grabbing a bite to eat, she's probably reading it on her phone. If Kate's at work, she's most likely reading it on a laptop or desktop computer. Basically, Kate went from reading a print newspaper sitting down inside a comfy room, to reading it across three devices, sometimes indoors, sometimes outdoors, sometimes at night, and sometimes during the day.

Remember, I didn't mention anything about Kate trying to fill out a form to renew her subscription or read instructions on how to send a letter to the editor; this use case is just for long-form reading. So, in this chapter you are going to learn how to identify common cross browser and device typographic issues that will cause problems for end users. Then I'll show you how to evaluate and test for those common issues in a browser on actual devices before development begins to avoid revisions.

The Typographic Choices You Actually Need to Test

OK, if you made it this far—and haven't cheated to get here by forgoing creating the necessary HTML and CSS pages in the previous section—you are ready to start evaluating your typographic choices and testing what you made in the browser. Prototyping tools give you the ability to create clickable mockups and make it easy to send a non-responsive .jpg version of your visual designs to view on a smartphone or tablet device. However, relying on these prototypes for accurate evaluation is problematic. For example, in **Figure 4.32**, the design in the screenshot on the left was created in Sketch specifically sized for the iPhone 7 Plus, viewed using the Sketch Mirror app on an iPhone 7 Plus. The image on the right was created specifically for the iPhone 4s, viewed on an iPhone 7 Plus. While not ideal, you can still estimate what your smaller sized designs will look like on a slightly larger screen. The same isn't true in reverse. In **Figure 4.33**, using the same software setup, the iPhone 4s sized artboard is on the left and the iPhone 7 Plus artboard is on the right. Since these are now both being viewed on an iPhone 4s, notice how the iPhone 7 Plus artboard on the right is significantly scaled, making it impossible to accurately evaluate your typographic choices.

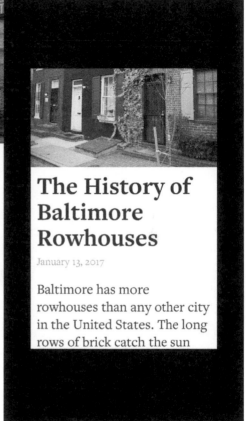

The History of Baltimore Rowhouses

January 13, 2017

Baltimore has more rowhouses than any other city in the United States. The long rows of brick catch the sun and seem to glow with that warmth we associate with home. Basement windows hold little dioramas with personal or religious themes, and painted screens turn narrow streets into outdoor art galleries.

A row house is much more than a line of attached homes. Before the advent of real estate speculation and planned developments, many homes were attached, forming rows. But a real rowhouse describes a large group of similar homes built at the same time by the same builder. The early 1900s saw large developments of these homes when builders created entire new neighborhoods.

The proliferation of these dwelling made Baltimore a city of homeowners. In the late 19th century, 70% of the population of the city owned their own homes. Practical, easy, and attractive

Figure 4.32

The History of Baltimore Rowhouses

January 13, 2017

Baltimore has more rowhouses than any other city in the United States. The long rows of brick catch the sun

The History of Baltimore Rowhouses

January 13, 2017

Baltimore has more rowhouses than any other city in the United States. The long rows of brick catch the sun and seem to glow with that warmth we associate with home. Basement windows hold little dioramas with personal or religious themes, and painted screens turn narrow streets into outdoor art galleries.

A row house is much more than a line of attached homes. Before the advent of real estate speculation and planned developments, many homes were attached, forming rows. But a real rowhouse describes a large group of similar homes built at the same time by the same builder. The early 1900s saw large developments of these homes when builders created entire new neighborhoods.

The proliferation of these dwelling made Baltimore a city of homeowners. In the late 19th century, 70% of the population of

Figure 4.33

If you wait until the front-end developer has coded the page to finally notice that the font is the wrong size on an actual device, it will cost you time and money to have the developer go back and make the necessary changes. Another short-coming of the prototyping programs is that you can't do any sort of performance testing. Depending on how the font was created and how you are delivering the fonts to a user's browser greatly affects how quickly they can begin reading your content. It's widely known that if a visitor to a website doesn't perceive that the website has the content they need within a second, they will abandon the page. Choosing the wrong fonts and delivery method could cause a site to not fully load for 4 or 5 seconds on a slow connection, which could cause your client to lose customers. This is a costly mistake, and one not quickly fixable once a website is live. Fortunately, these issues can be tested with the two different pages you just created in Part 01 of this chapter. The following is a list of common typographic issues you will face once your static mockups become live code. Learning to iden-tify these issues and testing them early in the design process will save you lots of time, money, and strained client relationships down the road.

Appearance

As it has already been alluded to, not all fonts are constructed equally, nor is every font designed for use on the screen. Just like Bell Centennial, designed by Matthew Carter, was designed to be printed at small sizes on paper specifically designed for phone books, there are many typefaces designed specifically for screen use. However, and herein lies the problem: there are a great many typefaces designed without a specific purpose. Just because you have a font installed on your computer doesn't necessarily mean it is intended to be viewed on a screen, so your job is to evaluate and test your fonts in the browser to ensure they are legible and performant.

Fortunately, it's a lot easier than you might think to get your fonts properly loaded into a webpage so you can evaluate them in different browsers and across a variety of devices. All that's really needed is the *Font Specimen Page* you created in the previous chapter to know if the font you picked is truly designed for the screen, and to make the necessary evaluations described below.

Font Size

As you are designing the layout of your webpage or app on your laptop or desktop computer in a layout program, you are already making a lot of bad assumptions—everyone has the same device and they will be viewing your designs in the same context you created them in. You're also probably assuming that a good quality font from a reputable type foundry has the same x-height and line-height (loosely the CSS equivalent for leading) between desktop fonts (OTF, TTF) and web fonts (EOT, WOFF, WOFF2, etc.), but this isn't always the case. Web fonts are specifically designed to be efficient for the user's browser to download and render quickly. Often times, well-designed web fonts include modifications to improve quality and/or avoid layout problems.

So, while the desktop font on your screen looks great at 18pt, and has the necessary apostrophes, acute accents, and other characters, once the front-end developer gets the web page built with actual web fonts things could look a lot different. That 18pt font could look more like 9pt with leading that makes the running text almost appear to be double spaced, and important special characters could be missing. Simply looking at the web version of your font in the browser will let you know if your choice is appropriate or if you need to make changes to your static mockups so the front-end developer will have accurate blueprints.

REAL WORLD EXAMPLES

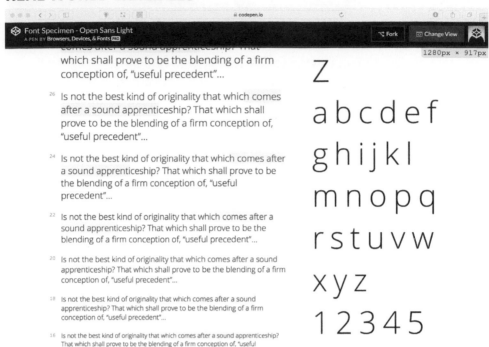

Figure 4.34

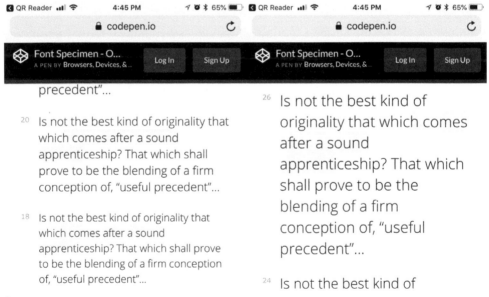

Figure 4.35

The 16 pixel font size in **Figure 4.34** looks like it's too small to read in a desktop sized browser. In **Figure 4.35** the 16 pixel font size looks like it could be a comfortable reading size for captions, or running text on a smartphone sized browser. However, the polar opposite is true. The 16 pixel font on a mobile device is nearly unreadable because it's so small even when held close, and the 24 pixel font size is a comfortable size for reading running text, even though it looks like it could be used for a headline or subheading. This is one reason why it's so critical to look at font size in the browser, and not rely on clickable prototypes, because they are often scaled to fit, and not actual size.

Note: The green highlights the character count of the reading line length between 45 and 75 characters, a good starting point for determining optimal line reading length based on the font's size and x-height. Using **Figure 4.34** as an example, a font-size between 22–26 pixels is the easiest for long form reading.

Font Weight

While you are evaluating the font size, you also want to be checking how the font weight renders on different devices and in different browsers. Many typefaces come in a variety of weights ranging from Ultra Thin to Extra Black. Unfortunately, different web browsers tend to render each weight differently enough that a font in Apple Safari may look different when viewed in Microsoft Edge, potentially making large chunks of running text difficult, if not impossible to read. While the biggest variation in how fonts are rendered happens between operating systems (i.e., Android, iOS, Mac, Windows, etc.), font weight also varies in browsers on the same operating system. You also need to be aware of the variation of how an OTF or TTF font is rendered by your desktop layout program when compared to how a WOFF is rendered by a web browser. Often times, a "regular" weight font is easily readable in your layout program but can almost appear as "semi-bold" when rendered by a web browser.

Depending on the primary end users, finding a font weight that is acceptable across all devices, browsers, and operating systems will be necessary. This is where a device emulator comes in handy. If you don't have one of the operating systems in your device lab, you can use an emulator to replicate what it would look like. While using the emulator is just an approximation, it will be enough of a clue to tell you if a font isn't rendering in the weight you expected and let you make adjustments. This is also where prototyping software fails! Even if you are looking at your properly sized artboard created on macOS on an Android device, the fonts were rendered by the layout program using desktop fonts, not by the browser using web fonts. Evaluating your choices this way will not give you an accurate indication of the web font's actual weight.

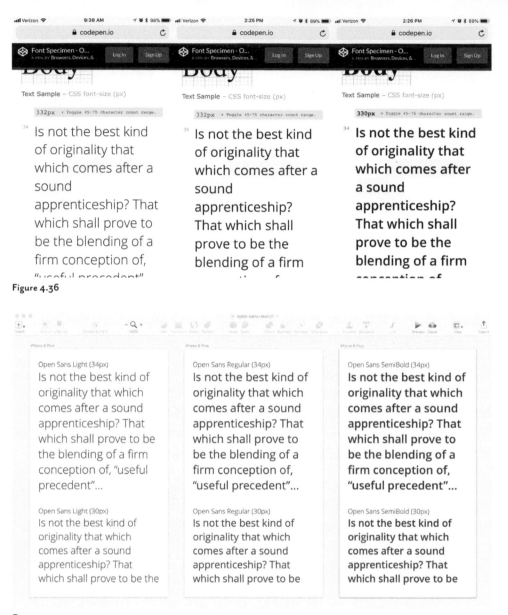

Figure 4.36

Figure 4.37

You can see the font family Open Sans renders slightly thicker in web browsers such as iOS Safari using WOFF **(Figure 4.36)** when compared to the same font family rendered in Sketch on macOS with TTF fonts **(Figure 4.37)**. Depending on end users and content you may want to go with Light and Semi-Bold instead of Regular and Bold.

Special Characters

If you look at the file size of a well-constructed desktop font that includes all the special characters, such as ligatures, lining, non-lining, and tabular numerals, acute accents, prime marks, etc., you'll see that it has a file size of 128k that can go upwards of 5mb. A font size this large will slow the performance of your website to a crawl (more details on this in the Performance section of this chapter). To avoid this, the conversion processes of OTF or TTF fonts to the WOFF format can potentially eliminate all those special characters to save file size, something you don't want to have happen. By viewing the font specimen page in a web browser, you can easily check to ensure that the specific features your visual designs need are supported. If they aren't supported you can find a new typeface long before the issue comes up in front-end development, or worse, when the site is live. You will notice that the .woff version of Chunk is missing the @ and the ' characters **(Figure 4.38)**. Both are important and commonly

Figure 4.38

used. Waiting until a website goes live to find out these characters are missing will cause a lot of unnecessary problems.

Contrast, User Settings, & Ambient Lighting

For the longest time, screens were stuck with a pixel density of 72 pixels per inch (ppi). This lower density mimicked print design in that you could use a pure black on white paper and there wouldn't be excessive contrast where it became difficult for the user to read for an extended period of time. Nowadays there are a lot of devices with stunningly high pixel densities such as Sony's Xperia Z5 boasting a density of 802 ppi, but more typical consumer smartphones come in the 300–400 ppi range such as the newer Apple iPhone and Google Pixel. Since there is such a high pixel density on modern screens, the contrast between pure black text (RGB 0, 0, 0) on a pure white (RGB 255, 255, 255) background puts a lot of strain on the user's eyes when they are doing a lot of reading. Instead of using a pure black against pure white, it's better to use a slightly lighter black such as RGB 38, 38, 38 or the hexadecimal equivalent #262626. Reducing the contrast of the running text no matter your color combinations will greatly reduce user's eye fatigue. However, reducing the contrast too much will also cause eye strain, especially for people with impaired vision or low resolution displays. Whatever black you do end up using will vary depending on the font you choose; #262626 is only a suggested starting point. You want to find the point where the text starts to look more like gray and then bring it back up until it looks black.

Another thing to check is the brightness settings. Users adjust the brightness settings to suit their viewing environment and personal tastes, and many devices attempt to change the brightness depending on available light automatically. Make sure the text is readable under a low brightness setting. Since CSS media queries can't use a device's sensor yet[6] to detect what type of lighting environment the user is currently in, the best you can do is evaluate your font choices to see if they hold up for the extremes such as high and low contrast. If the readability of the font doesn't hold up well, pick a font that does.

While you can't plan for every possible way a user is going to interact with your design, you can hedge your bets and check for some common features such as "Night Mode," when text becomes white on a black background. While this may be specific to eBooks and apps, it's good practice to check if your typographic choices are still easily readable when the running text is reversed to black on white for web projects too, even if that's not your intention.

Hierarchy

If properly marked up with HTML tags, text that appears on a website will have a default visual hierarchy. While search engines such as Google and Bing can easily read the HTML tags to help users find your products and services, the default styling of these HTML elements can make it difficult for users to clearly distinguish between headlines, subheads, and the start of a new section. Each font may have its own scale that's different from the other fonts you may be using in the layout of which all may vary widely from the compressed WOFF web font seen in the browser compared to the OTF or TTF version you are using in your layout program. This is where the typographic hierarchy page you created in the previous chapter will come in handy. You can load the different fonts you will be using in the page and see where you will need to adjust the default hierarchy.

---

6   W3C, 2017. Detecting the ambient light level: the light-level feature. https://drafts.csswg.org/mediaqueries-5/#light-level (accessed April 27, 2018).

Line Height

Line height—leading in the print design world and `line-height` in actual CSS—is the space between each line of text. It's very important to check that the line-height of your desktop font looks like you are expecting it to as a web font. Since not all fonts are created equal, there is the possibility that the line-height of the font on your MAC or PC is different than the web version, which could throw off your design once it's in development. To adjust the line-height in your font specimen page or typographic hierarchy page add the following CSS property and value to the body tag.

```
body {
    line-height: 1.35;
}
```

The CSS property doesn't use a value like ems or pixels, rather it uses a unitless value. Try adjusting it from as low as .5 to as much as 3 or more **(Figures 4.39 & 4.40)** to see how line-height affects the hierarchy until you find the ideal amount of line-height for easy reading of your running text. Generally, narrower columns of text require less line-height and wider columns require more.

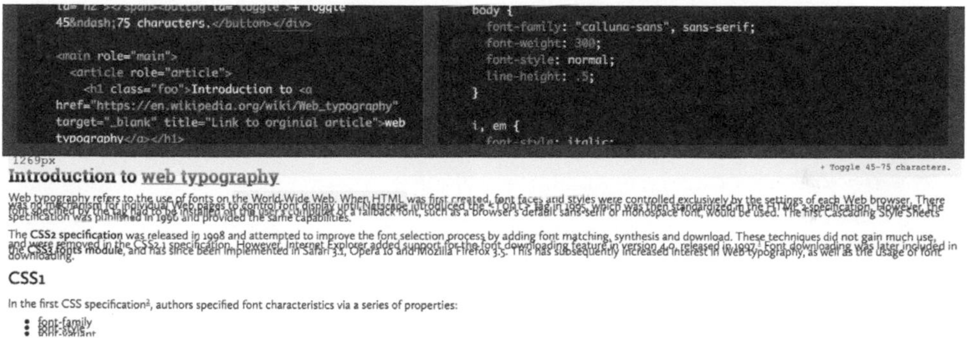

Figure 4.39

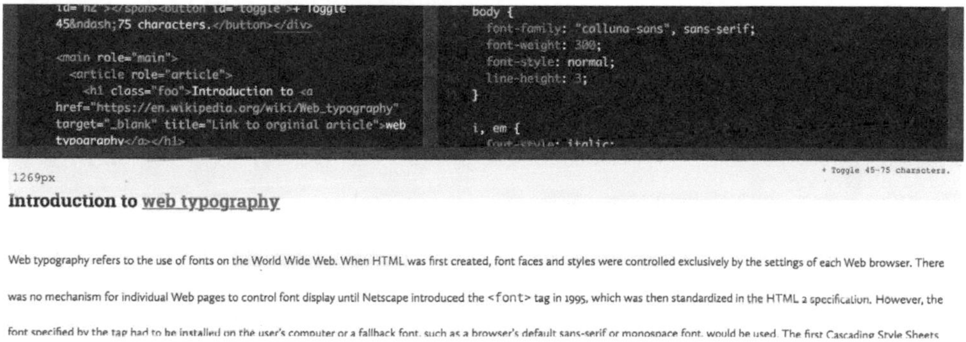

Figure 4.40

Headlines and Subheadings

Line-height of headlines and subheadings needs to be set differently than the running text in your typographic hierarchy page. Since the line-height scales automatically with the font size, the headlines and subheadings generally have too much line-height if the text were to wrap to a second line, making the single headline appear as two sentences **(Figure 4.41)**. To adjust the line-height for the headings, simply add the following CSS declarations to your <h1> through <h6> tags and adjust each accordingly **(Figure 4.42)** until you get the exact line-height that is the easiest for the user to read.

```
h1 {
    line-height: 1.1;
}
```

Figure 4.41

Figure 4.42

Now that you have adjusted the line-height for your headings and subheadings, there is still a little more work to do. While the default spacing between the <h1> and <p> tags may look adequate for the main headline on the page, you still need to consider the spacing between paragraphs and subheadings. Line-height doesn't control that spacing; rather, it's controlled by the CSS margin property, and not just margin on the <h1> tag, but on the <p> tag as well. However, before I show you how to adjust the spacing let's look at the difference between a subheading that doesn't have adjusted margins and one that does.

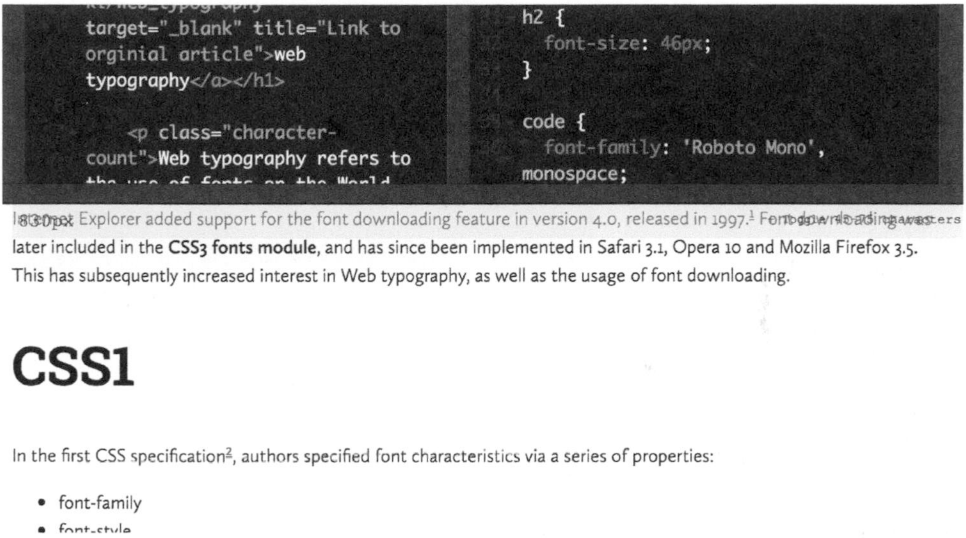

```
target="_blank" title="Link to
orginial article">web
typography</a></h1>

    <p class="character-
count">Web typography refers to
the use of fonts on the World
```
```
h2 {
    font-size: 46px;
}

code {
    font-family: 'Roboto Mono',
monospace;
```

Internet Explorer added support for the font downloading feature in version 4.0, released in 1997.[1] Font downloading was later included in the **CSS3 fonts module**, and has since been implemented in Safari 3.1, Opera 10 and Mozilla Firefox 3.5. This has subsequently increased interest in Web typography, as well as the usage of font downloading.

CSS1

In the first CSS specification[2], authors specified font characteristics via a series of properties:

- font-family
- font-style

Figure 4.43

```
<h2>CSS1</h2>

    <p>In the first CSS
specification<sup><a href="#ref-
002">2</a></sup>, authors
specified font characteristics
via a series of properties:</p>

    <ul>
```
```
h2 {
    font-size: 46px;
    margin-bottom: 0;
}

h2 + p {
    margin-top: 0;
}
```

synthesis and download. These techniques did not gain much use, and were removed in the CSS2.1 specification. However, Internet Explorer added support for the font downloading feature in version 4.0, released in 1997.[1] Font downloading was later included in the **CSS3 fonts module**, and has since been implemented in Safari 3.1, Opera 10 and Mozilla Firefox 3.5. This has subsequently increased interest in Web typography, as well as the usage of font downloading.

CSS1

In the first CSS specification[2], authors specified font characteristics via a series of properties:

- font-family
- font-style

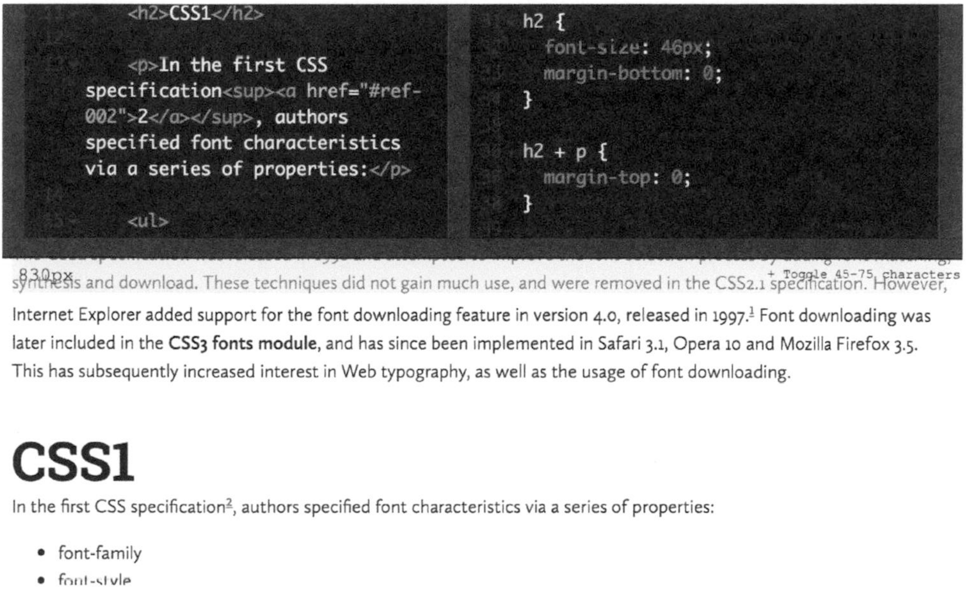

Figure 4.44

In **Figure 4.43** you can see on the left that the CSS1 subheading wrapped in an <h2> tag appears to be floating between the two paragraphs. A typical top to bottom western reading order would suggest that the subheading is the start of a new section, but if there was a longer section title it could appear almost as a pull quote instead and give no visual association to the surrounding running text. In **Figure 4.44** the margin has been adjusted on both the headline tag and the paragraph tag that immediately follows it. This helps the reader better associate the running text to the section title.

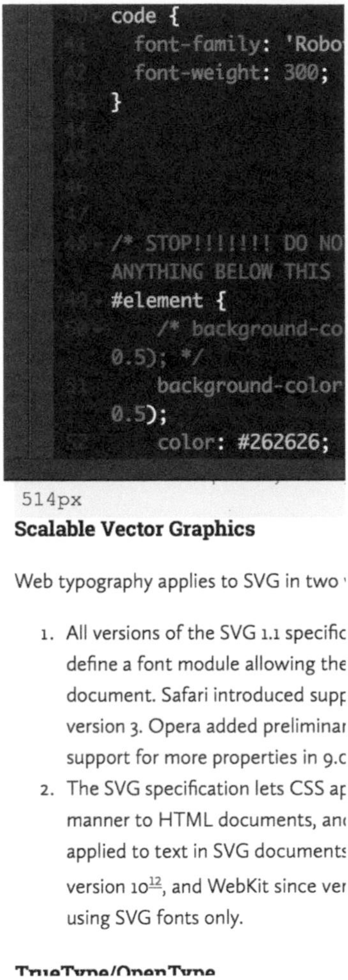

```
code {
    font-family: 'Robo
    font-weight: 300;
}




/* STOP!!!!!!! DO NO
ANYTHING BELOW THIS
#element {
    /* background-co
0.5); */
    background-color
0.5);
    color: #262626;
```

```
h2 + p {
    margin-top: 0;
}

ol {
    list-style-type: decimal-leading-zero;
    padding-left: 2em;
}

code {
    font-family: 'Roboto Mono', monospace;
    font-weight: 300;
}
```

514px
Scalable Vector Graphics

514px   + Toggle 45-75 char
Scalable Vector Graphics

Web typography applies to SVG in two

Web typography applies to SVG in two ways:

1. All versions of the SVG 1.1 specific
   define a font module allowing the
   document. Safari introduced supp
   version 3. Opera added preliminar
   support for more properties in 9.0
2. The SVG specification lets CSS ap
   manner to HTML documents, and
   applied to text in SVG documents
   version 10[12], and WebKit since ver
   using SVG fonts only.

01. All versions of the SVG 1.1 specification, including the SVGT subs
    define a font module allowing the creation of fonts within an SV(
    document. Safari introduced support for many of these propertie
    version 3. Opera added preliminary support in version 8.0, with
    support for more properties in 9.0.
02. The SVG specification lets CSS apply to SVG documents in a sim
    manner to HTML documents, and the @font-face rule can be ap
    to text in SVG documents. Opera added support for this in versic
    10[12], and WebKit since version 325 also supports this method usin
    SVG fonts only.

TrueType/OpenType
Figure 4.45

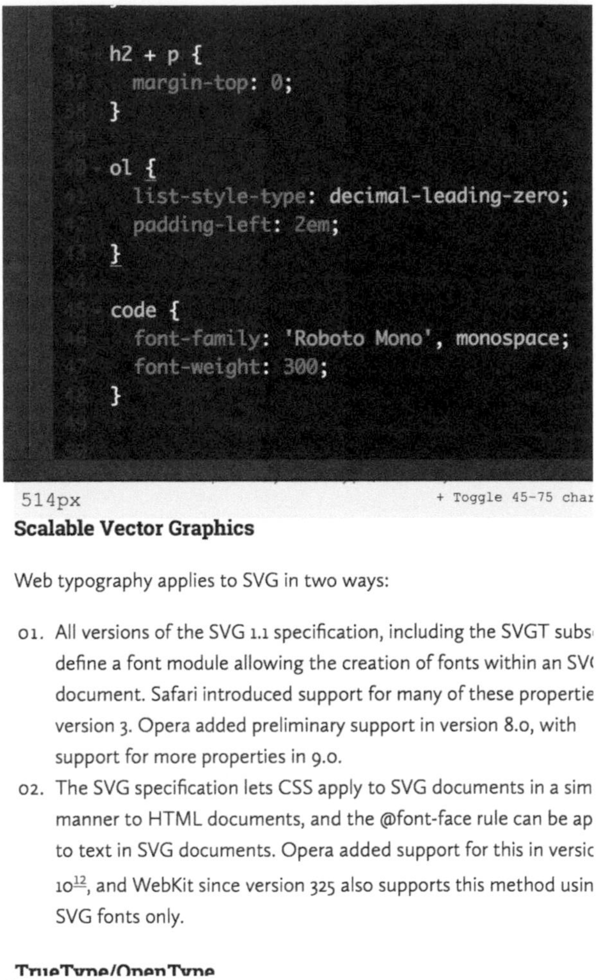

TrueType/OpenType
Figure 4.46

Ordered and Unordered Lists

Ordered and unordered lists come with some default styling that makes it hard to distinguish one bulleted item from another. You can also make the argument that the lists aren't indented enough or are indented too much. Again, you can evaluate them in the browser instead of as a static mockup, so you truly know how your lists are going to look once the site is live.

In **Figure 4.45** you can see the default styling of the list. In **Figure 4.46** you can see how adding leading zeros to the numbers helps keep them evenly aligned. To accommodate the extra numeral CSS padding is added. I used an em unit for this example, which is out of the norm for this book, and the manner I'm using it in my not be front-end development best practice with the ch CSS unit available and supported in modern browsers. If you want to learn more about other units of measure that your front-end developer will use, such as rems and viewport units, I'd recommend checking out the CSS-Tricks website for some examples and short tutorials.[7,8,9] Finally, you'll notice that when there is a lot of text for each bullet it's hard to tell when one numbered item begins and another one ends **(Figure 4.47)**. By adding a little extra margin to the bottom of each list item it becomes easier to read. You can see the final adjusted version on the right.

To adjust your own ordered and unordered lists simply add the following to your forked pen or downloaded files and adjust each em unit accordingly to preference.

```
ul {
    padding-left: 4em;
}

ul li {
    margin-bottom: .75em;
}
```

Or

```
ol {
    list-style-type: decimal-leadir
    padding-left: 2em;
}

ol li {
    margin-bottom: .75em;
}

code {
    font-family: 'Roboto Mono', mor
```

514px   + Togg

Scalable Vector Graphics

Web typography applies to SVG in two ways:

01. All versions of the SVG 1.1 specification, including th define a font module allowing the creation of fonts ' document. Safari introduced support for many of th version 3. Opera added preliminary support in versio support for more properties in 9.0.

02. The SVG specification lets CSS apply to SVG docum manner to HTML documents, and the @font-face rι to text in SVG documents. Opera added support for 10^{12}, and WebKit since version 325 also supports this SVG fonts only.

TrueType/OpenType
Figure 4.47

7   Coyier, Chris. 2012. Viewport Sized Typography. https://css-tricks.com/viewport-sized-typography/ (accessed April 23, 2018).
8   Shadeed, Ahmad. 2016. Building Resizeable Components with Relative CSS Units. https://css-tricks.com/building-resizeable-components-relative-css-units/ (accessed April 23, 2018).
9   Graham, Geoff. 2017. Fluid Typography. https://css-tricks.com/snippets/css/fluid-typography/ (accessed April 23, 2018).

```
ol {
    list-style-type: decimal-leading-zero;
    padding-left: 4em;
}

ol li {
    margin-bottom: .75em;
}
```

The *Typographic Hierarchy Evaluation* and *Font Specimen* pages give you just enough information to evaluate your visual design choices for mockup in a layout program like Sketch. While you could easily create this visual hierarchy in your layout program, it's better to give your front-end developer specific instructions instead of general ones. To use a print design analogy, giving the front-end developer actual HTML and CSS instructions is parallel to specifying Pantone 270U ink printed on Classic Crest Natural White 110# cover to your commercial printer instead of specifying purple ink on white card stock. While both are technically the same, the specific instructions will get you exactly what you want not an approximation. In Chapter 06 I demonstrate how to turn the *Typographic Hierarchy Evaluation* page into a typographic design system that could be used for actual production.

Performance

Have you ever visited a website that took forever to load? You probably watched a blank white screen magically change when an image or colored background flashed in. Then you started to see text appear, in chunks, but then the chunks of text started jumping around as image after image popped up throughout the page. Once the page was more or less rendered in the browser you had your content jump around once again to accommodate the slow loading advertisements if you weren't using an ad blocker. Finally, now that everything is in place and you are ready to start reading the article or shopping for your friend's birthday, the font suddenly changes from something like Arial to a custom font. Being able to physically watch a website build isn't a good user experience, and an experience that users won't tolerate. This slow to load website is a result of poor design choices that can be exacerbated by poor front-end development and web server setup.

I left internet speed out of that last statement on purpose. We are not going to blame slow internet speeds for any of this because diligent planning and performance minded design choices will overcome a slow 3G connection during a high-use time, such as standing in the middle of New York's Times Square on New Year's Eve. This is an extreme performance edge case, but if your design choices work under an extreme circumstance, they will perform beautifully under ideal conditions.

If you are designing a native iOS or Android app, or an eBook, the fonts probably won't cause slow performance because they are usually embedded within the application and don't need to be downloaded by the browser. If you are using fonts on a website, each font you ask your user to load slows the performance of the site down considerably. This is a gross generalization, but a single weight and style of a font is around 30kb each. If you use 6 different font weights and styles at 30kb each, that comes to 180kb. The average download speed of a 3G connection is about 600kb per second and 4G LTE is about 3000kb per second. If your website doesn't contain any images, excessive amounts of running text (think of long-form reading like articles), JavaScript enhancements, or analytics tracking, your fonts will download in just under a second and most likely be viewable within a second, and fully rendered within two seconds.

Now throw an overly optimized hero image onto the website at 120kb, a few additional optimized images at 40kb each, a logo at 10kb, the actual HTML and CSS files easily reaching a combined 50kb, and a JavaScript file necessary to add some functions to the website at 15kb. This super slim webpage is now at 495kb if you only have three well-optimized images, one hero image, and logo. At 500kb you are dangerously close to having more content than can be downloaded with a reliable 3G connection within the average 1 second until a user abandons the site. You're better off going with a single headline font, a regular weight, an italic, and a bold font. If you don't believe page bloat caused by poor design choices is an issue, it's been calculated that the average web page clocks in at 2.2MB. A 2.2MB page would take over 2 seconds just to download on a 4G network running at maximum speed. That doesn't include time for the browser to render the page. Since you only have 1 second to engage the user, you're already sunk. Also worth consideration: instead of relying on images that can only be used once, try to rely more on fonts and CSS to add visual interest – they are often smaller files than images and can be reused in infinite configurations without reducing performance.

Fortunately, you can easily run tests to evaluate some of your design choices for performance. To conduct the tests, your files will need to be on a remote web server. So, you don't have to purchase a web hosting account, you can upload your typographic hierarchy page to the performance test server provided on the book's website discussed in Chapter 03 *Setting Up Your Toolbox*. Once you've uploaded the files and run the tests, you will learn how to evaluate the results in the upcoming section.

Running a Webpage Test

The Webpage Test is a valuable tool to evaluate your design choices. Not only can you test how long it will take your designs to load in different situations, it also gives you a snapshot every 10th of a second showing what your site looks like while it's being downloaded and rendered. It even gives you a chart to better understand what files are causing the page to render slowly. Best of all, the tool is free and simple to use. There is a lot of documentation on how to use Webpage Test to its fullest, and I've already covered the basics on running a test in Chapter 03 *Setting Up Your Toolbox*, so I'll stick to discussing what you should be evaluating for, optimization, not the steps necessary to run the actual test.

HOW TO INTERPRET THE RESULTS

The real key to this isn't the Load Time, it's the *Time Until First View*. The user doesn't have to have the website completely loaded in one second, rather they need to feel assured within a second that they will get the results they came to the site looking for. You want to look at the timeline to see what the user will see at ½ a second, at 1 second, at 1½ seconds, 2 seconds, etc.

In this test, I used Open Sans Condensed Bold for the headlines and subheadings, and Open Sans Light, Light Italic, and Semi-bold for the running text, both hosted by Google Fonts **(Figure 4.48)**. That's a modest 4 fonts weighing in around 100kb combined.

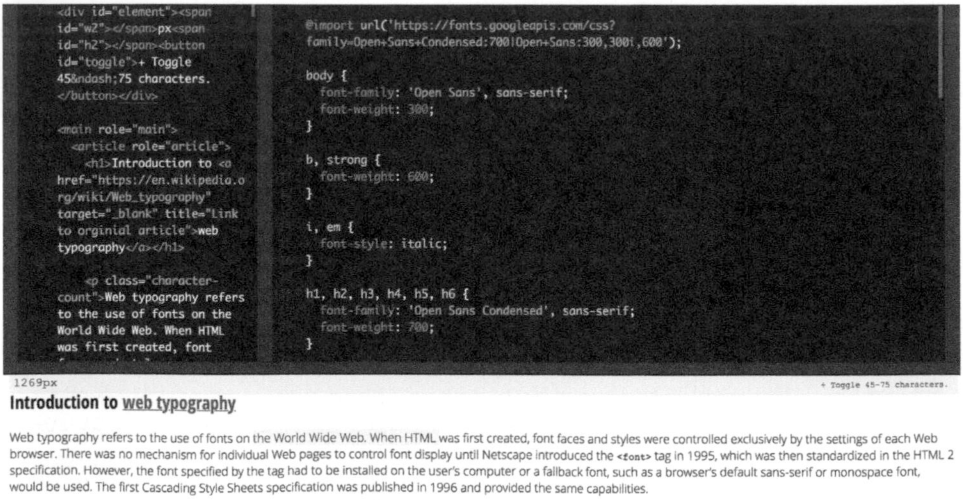
<div id="element"><span id="w2"></span>px<span id="h2"></span><button id="toggle">+ Toggle 45–75 characters.</button></div>
<main role="main">
<article role="article">
<h1>Introduction to <a href="https://en.wikipedia.org/wiki/Web_typography" target="_blank" title="Link to orginial article">web typography</a></h1>
<p class="character-count">Web typography refers to the use of fonts on the World Wide Web. When HTML was first created, font
@import url('https://fonts.googleapis.com/css?family=Open+Sans+Condensed:700|Open+Sans:300,300i,600');
body {
font-family: 'Open Sans', sans-serif;
font-weight: 300;
}
b, strong {
font-weight: 600;
}
i, em {
font-style: italic;
}
h1, h2, h3, h4, h5, h6 {
font-family: 'Open Sans Condensed', sans-serif;
font-weight: 700;
}
1269px
+ Toggle 45-75 characters.
Introduction to web typography
Web typography refers to the use of fonts on the World Wide Web. When HTML was first created, font faces and styles were controlled exclusively by the settings of each Web browser. There was no mechanism for individual Web pages to control font display until Netscape introduced the <font> tag in 1995, which was then standardized in the HTML 2 specification. However, the font specified by the tag had to be installed on the user's computer or a fallback font, such as a browser's default sans-serif or monospace font, would be used. The first Cascading Style Sheets specification was published in 1996 and provided the same capabilities.

Figure 4.48

In **Figure 4.49** the time until first view comes in around 1.3 seconds which, in theory, isn't bad. However, click on the "Filmstrip View" to see what your user sees in real time!

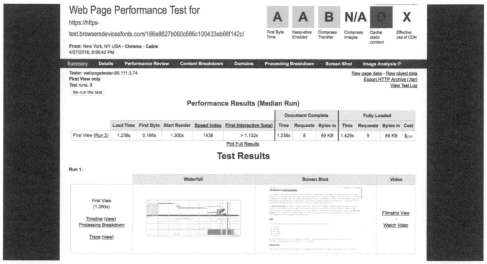

Figure 4.49

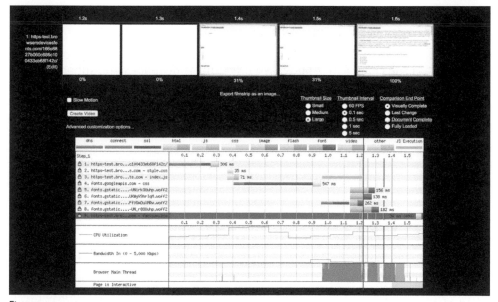

Figure 4.50

Figure 4.50 demonstrates that in reality the user sees a blank screen for 1.4 seconds until the text flashes in. The reason for the wait? It's the fonts! The browser is stopping the rendering of the page content until the fonts load which doesn't happen for 1.3 seconds on a fast internet connection.

Using the same index.html file for content, I removed all the CSS declarations that load the custom fonts and reran the test and got much different results, loading within .6 seconds using native system fonts **(Figure 4.51)**.

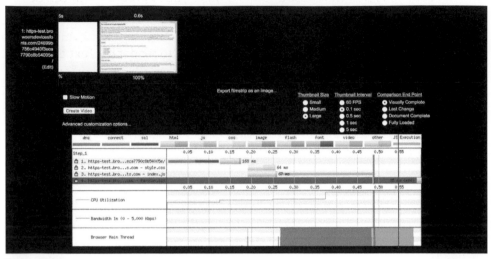

Figure 4.51

TIPS

Depending on the results of your own tests, you may want to limit your font choices to one or two weights. Think of each font in the context of "Bang for your buck." If a font is only used once in a design, it's not delivering value. To leverage this, consider using a system font for your headlines. Since the headline font will be used sparingly, you aren't getting a "good bang for your buck." Using a system font for your headlines paired with a custom font for the running text will improve performance while enhancing readability. If you really want to make a difference in your design's performance, try using some of the newer system fonts discussed in the upcoming section for all the text in your designs to really speed things up.

FOUT, FOIT, FOFT, and Fallbacks?

Flash of Unstyled Text (FOUT), Flash of Invisible Text (FOIT), and Flash of Faux Text (FOFT) aren't terms I made up. They are real situations that can adversely affect how your users view your webpage designs. What exactly do FOUT, FOIT, and FOFT look like to the user? Have you ever visited a website and seen the fonts quickly flash from something like Arial and Georgia to another custom font? How about not seeing any text at all and then all of a sudden, the text just magically appears? Things like this are caused when the web browser has to stop rendering the page while it waits for the font that isn't installed on the user's computer to be downloaded from a remote web server. On a slow internet connection, this can cause the user to abandon your site. Your front-end developer will have some strategies to avoid these problems, and perhaps, in a couple of years this might not be a problem at all. For now, there is a potential solution that your front-end developer may recommend that will cause another problem, but a problem that can be strategically controlled.

In layman's terms, it's possible to tell the web browser to render the text on a page using a system font such as Georgia or Verdana that is already installed on most mobile devices and computers, and then re-render the page with the custom font once it's finished being downloaded to the user's computer from the remote web server. This lets the entire page render, instead of it stopping and waiting for the font to download. However, this creates another issue I'm sure you have experienced. Have you ever visited a website, started reading and scrolling, only for the page to jump around causing you to lose your place? This is usually caused by a system font being initially loaded that doesn't have a similar x-height and line-height or, more often, width proportions to the custom font loaded later.

To solve this, make sure your system font matches the line-height, width, and x-height of the custom font and pass that information along to your front-end developer. Now your system font will load with CSS instructions telling it what the size and line-height needs to be, so it matches the custom font once it's finished loading. Once the custom font is downloaded, the user will see the font style change, but since they now have a similar size, there will be minimal text reflow preventing users from losing their place. Exactly how you technically achieve this is a bit complicated and best left up to the front-end developer. You just need to give CSS instructions so both fonts match line-height, width, and x-height.

1280px × 510px

Raleway

Size Comparison

Raleway   Verdana   Georgia   Arial   Times

Body **Body** Body **Body** Body

Figure 4.52

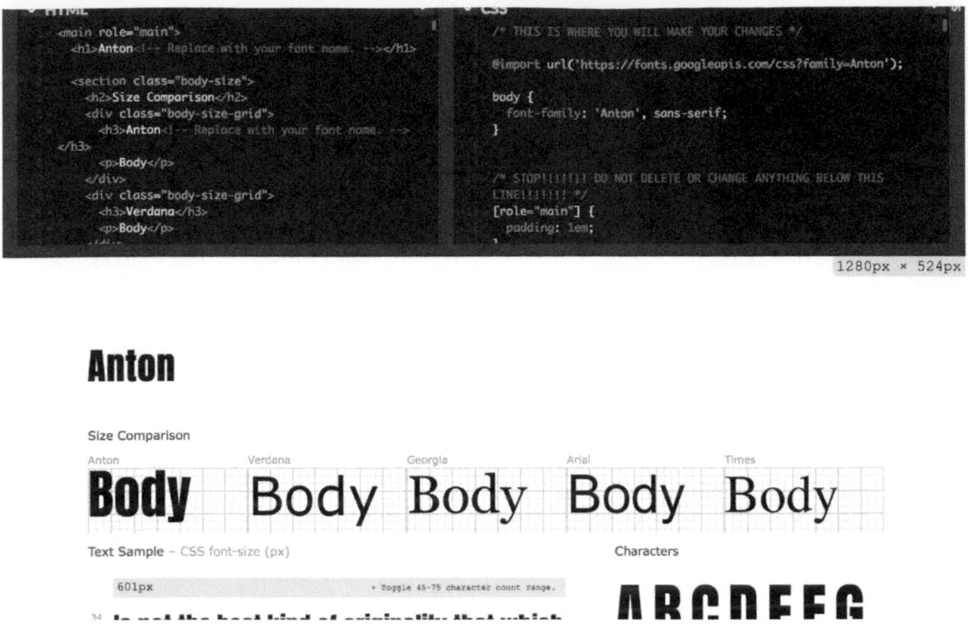

```
HTML
<main role="main">
  <h1>Anton<!-- Replace with your font name. --></h1>

  <section class="body-size">
    <h2>Size Comparison</h2>
    <div class="body-size-grid">
      <h3>Anton<!-- Replace with your font name. -->
    </h3>
      <p>Body</p>
    </div>
    <div class="body-size-grid">
      <h3>Verdana</h3>
      <p>Body</p>
```

```
CSS
/* THIS IS WHERE YOU WILL MAKE YOUR CHANGES */

@import url('https://fonts.googleapis.com/css?family=Anton');

body {
  font-family: 'Anton', sans-serif;
}

/* STOP!!!!!!! DO NOT DELETE OR CHANGE ANYTHING BELOW THIS
LINE!!!!!!! */
[role="main"] {
  padding: 1em;
```

1280px × 524px

Anton

Size Comparison

Anton	Verdana	Georgia	Arial	Times
Body	Body	Body	Body	Body

Text Sample – CSS font-size (px)   Characters

601px   + Toggle 45–75 character count range.

ABCDEFG

Figure 4.53

To help you visualize the effect I'm describing, I'm using the Body Size Comparison section of the *Font Specimen Page* to compare two fonts—Raleway and Anton—both available from Google Fonts. In **Figure 4.52** you will notice that by default, the x-height of Raleway is similar to common system fonts. Since they are the same overall size, users will avoid seeing that awkward reflowing of text I described earlier. In **Figure 4.53** you will notice that the x-height of Anton is much bigger than the common system fonts with the same 70px font size. To avoid major text reflowing when using Anton, it will need to have a smaller font size. It is important to note that everything I just demonstrated isn't an exact science. How your front-end developer chooses to solve this problem will change as technologies change.

Updated System Fonts

More and more of the new system fonts that Android, Apple, Microsoft, and others have created for their operating systems are becoming easy to read and provide much needed variation to the web safe stalwarts of Arial, Georgia, Times New Roman, and Verdana. Best of all, since they are already installed on the device, they don't affect site performance. Many popular publishing platforms such as the WordPress admin panel already utilize these new generations of system fonts to ensure quick performance. You can try them for yourself in the Font Specimen or Typographic Hierarchy pages you already created by adding the following line to the CSS panel or file (**Figure 4.54**).

```
body {
    font-family: -apple-system, BlinkMacSystemFont, "Seg-
oe UI", Roboto, Helvetica, Arial, sans-serif, "Apple Color
Emoji", "Segoe UI Emoji", "Segoe UI Symbol";
}
```

Figure 4.54

With just two simple HTML pages and a tiny bit of CSS and web font knowledge, you can accurately make a majority of your typographic design decisions long before front-end development begins. While these extra steps may seem cumbersome at first, it will quickly become second nature if you make it a part of regular design workflow. Think of this step as you are beginning to create a branding guide to give to your clients at the end of the project. Don't delete the files you just created, you need to save them to hand off to your front-developer, discussed in detail in Chapter 06 *Style Guides for Everyone*. Finally, while each front-end developer has her own working method and may want different deliverables from you, simply giving them access to these pages will be a head start to accurately developing your design vision.

Finding Breakpoints for Text & Images

As in the previous chapters, you can choose between the browser based or Native Application based workflow. However, since you will be working with images in this chapter, it will be necessary to upgrade to a CodePen Pro subscription to follow along with the demos.

If you have decided by this point that the Browser based workflow isn't for you, skip straight to the Native Application based workflow demos, because you won't be able to follow along with the ones written for CodePen without a paid subscription. You will need the following regardless of which testing workflow you plan on using.

- Photoshop or Affinity Photo

- ImageOptim https://imageoptim.com *macOS only*

- or JPEG & PNG Stripper http://www.steelbytes.com/?mid=30 *Windows Only*

Preparing Images for the Web

As a design educator, instructing the proper preparation of images for use on the web has got to be one of my biggest sources of frustration. Too many times I have seen web projects using 5MB .jpg images that must have been pulled directly off a camera. This also happens on many portfolio websites as images of work are converted into unwieldy file sizes that take forever to download. Aside from the obvious "not paying attention" to what I'm saying during class, I think students and graphic designers in general struggle with images because they don't fully understand how images affect the usability of a website as they work from their laptop instead of a web server, and there isn't a clear, concise process to optimize images.

Teaching the image optimization process only got worse once smartphones became the predominant method to consume web-based content, and new HTML elements gave designers the ability to art direct how images are best cropped to fill the browser windows based on the size of a device. There is some good news however: you don't have to be a front-end developer to test out your image choices. In this section you will learn just enough about image optimization methods, and the minimal amount of HTML and CSS necessary to test and evaluate your design choices as live web pages. This will let you quickly decide if your visual design choices are going to be problematic long before you get the front-end developer involved.

This may sound like it's going to be an entire chapter about images. Fear not. While I cover a great deal about how images affect layout in this chapter, typography is discussed too. To make some additional typographic choices that I have not covered yet, all your content needs to be in the browser. This means images and text in gridded layouts. Since I have already covered typographic choices that can be made without the context of layout, I'm going to discuss images first and later put them both together for you to evaluate and test. One final note before I get into the details. It's worth mentioning that the repeating mantras of this chapter will be "There is no one right way to do this," and "Work with your front-end developer to determine the best method." The goal of this chapter is really meant to get you to test and evaluate your design choices early on to limit performance issues caused by your visual design choices once it's too late.

Picking the Optimal Image File Type

There are four image formats currently that all modern web browsers will display inline on a web page: the Graphics Interchange Format or .gif, Joint Photographic Experts Group or .jpg/jpeg, Portable Network Graphics or .png, and Scalable Vector Graphics or .svg. None of these formats is better than the other. Rather, they all serve a different function, but with the same shared goal of making the smallest possible file size. There is already a lot written about the different formats, so I'm not going to go into detail about the history or other specifics of these file types. Rather, I'm just going to give you a general overview of each that will hopefully be enough to guide you in deciding which format to pick for your own tests and evaluations.

Graphics Interchange Format .gif

The lossy (loses image quality) .gif format works to optimize file size by reducing the number of colors in an image. By default, the maximum number of colors a .gif can support is 256. A 600 × 600 pixel .gif with 256 colors will be a much larger file size than a 600 × 600 pixel .gif with only 16 colors. Since the .gif removes color information, it does a poor job of optimizing continuous tone photographs. This is why most animated .gifs look very grainy. Gifs are best suited for icons and illustrations with limited color palettes and details.

Joint Photographic Experts Group .jpg/.jpeg

The lossy (loses image quality) .jpg format works to optimize file size by finding similar colors in an image then taking those two colors and combining them into one and replacing the original colors in the image with the newly created color. By turning two similar colors into a single averaged color, there is less pixel information in the image, and the file size becomes smaller. The .jpg format works best with photographs with lots of detail. When done correctly, image file size can be reduced quite significantly while maintaining the original visual integrity. When too much .jpg compression is applied you will get the pixilation also known as artifacting. Artifacting occurs when multiple similar colored pixels are combined into a single color. Those singular pixels now become a big enough block to be seen by the eye in a continuous tone image.

Portable Network Graphics .png

PNG-8

The PNG-8 format is very similar to the .gif file, with a slightly smaller file size. It's best suited for icons and simple illustrations. It only supports a maximum of 256 colors, but with better transparency support. However, unlike the .gif, PNG animation doesn't have full modern browser support.

PNG-24

The PNG-24 is a lossless file compression format that offers the ability to preserve a full range of transparency, unlike GIF which only offers 1-bit all-or-nothing transparency. It's compression method works by examining a single pixel and its neighboring pixels. Instead of storing information for each pixel—in an oversimplification of the process—it stores the complete information of the single pixel, and the differences between original and neighboring pixels. This compression method reduces the file size, without losing image quality, but it doesn't reduce the file sizes of continuous tone images (photographs) as much as .jpg compression. Because of the nature of the PNG-24 compression, it's suited for detailed illustrations and some photographic images.

Scalable Vector Graphic .svg

The lossless .svg format is related to the .eps file format in how it stores information. However, the .svg file format supports additional capabilities and features useful for web design such as animation, compression, styling with CSS, and more. Basically, a .svg stores plot points—better known as nodes—as a list of coordinates with information on how to visually display those nodes. Much like the .gif, the .svg is ideal for icons and illustrations but with two distinct advantages.

The first advantage is .svg images are infinitely scalable without any image degradation. This is extremely important as high-density (retina) displays are now the norm. The higher resolution of high-density devices makes bitmapped images problematic in that to keep them looking crisp in high-resolution devices, they need to be almost double in size.

The second advantage is that .svg images are capable of being animated and visually styled through CSS and other means. This allows for a single .svg image to be used across an entire website with substantially different variations when visually appropriate.

Picking the Optimal Image Size

Reducing the pixel dimensions of a photographic image will usually yield the biggest reduction in file size. For example, a 4608 × 3456 pixel .jpg straight from my camera is 7.2 MB. That same image resized to 2880 × 2160 pixels—the resolution of a 15" MacBook Pro—without compression is 4.1 MB. Finally, that same image resized to 1024 × 768—the resolution of many tablet devices—without compression is just under 1 MB.

Unfortunately, simply resizing an image isn't as straightforward as it once was. Prior to 2007 and the introduction of smartphones you could confidently predict that most users had something in the neighborhood of 1024 × 768, 72 pixels per inch (ppi) resolution monitor. If you were designing on a 12 column grid you could get a precise image size, and know upfront how long it would take for that image to load. Now with the introduction of smartphones, tablets, laptops, gaming consoles, and smart TVs it is impossible to predict the type of device your website will be viewed on, and therefore it's impossible to pick an appropriate image size.

To make matters worse, as briefly introduced in Chapter 04 *Typography*, monitors are no longer relegated to 72 ppi. An Apple 15" MacBook Pro is 220 ppi and a Microsoft Surface Pro is 267 ppi. This means that a 600 pixel wide image at 72 ppi would have to be 1833 pixels wide on the MacBook Pro and 2225 pixels wide on the Surface Pro to appear the same size as the image would appear on the 1024 × 768, 72 ppi device without any artifacting. Fortunately, HTML5 and CSS3 have a lot of methods for delivering the properly sized image for whichever device the user happens to be viewing your website on.

While utilizing HTML5 and CSS3 to deliver the optimal image to the end user falls under the purview of the front-end developer, as a designer you still need to conduct tests and evaluations on your visual design choices to determine early on if what you are doing will be performant. Fortunately, you can get enough data to analyze your design choices by creating a couple of simple test pages tailored to a couple of size ranges. Keeping in mind while there is no best practices way to determine optimal image sizes, with a little research and strategic thought, you can at least come up with a decent analog to how your visual design choices will perform as live websites.

Website Analytics

When approaching a website redesign, visual designers tend to overlook the research component of the redesign process and jump right into the visual design process. However, this approach is a critical misstep. Simply looking at the analytics of a website will help you better understand your audience. For this example, I've included some basic stats from the Design Edu Today website that I personally designed and developed. Looking over the course of a few months, the site has had 19,564 unique visitors. Of those unique visitors, 17,796 visited on a desktop device, 1,529 on a mobile device, and 239 on a tablet device. Based on the numbers, I really need to make sure that the desktop experience is performant, but not at the expense of the mobile device users.

A closer look at those numbers revealed that of the 17,796 desktop visitors, 3,286 had a screen resolution of 1024 × 768 pixels, 1,793 had a screen resolution of 2560 × 1440 pixels, 1,053 had a screen resolution of 1440 × 900 pixels, and 666 had a screen resolution of 1920 × 1080 pixels. The most popular screen size for the 1,529 mobile visitors was 375 × 667 pixels, coming from an iPhone.

Based on these statistics, I'm going to test two different image sizes, basically, the extremes. I'm going to test images that will look good at the larger 2560 × 1440 pixels, and the smaller 375 × 667 pixels. Knowing that most iPhones have higher pixel densities, it will take a 750 pixel wide image to look crisp on a 375 pixel wide high density display. While it's most likely that the 2560 × 1440 pixel desktop devices have a much higher pixel density than 72 dpi, the majority of my visitors have a resolution of 1024 pixels wide, so an image at 2560 pixels wide will look really crisp on the smaller desktop devices.

For this demo I'm going to make the general assumption—based on researching the website's statistics—that I need to map out my images based on a user's device being either 750 or 2560 pixels wide. For the sake of this demo, I suggest you follow along with my examples, but when it comes time for you to start incorporating this method of testing and evaluating into your own workflow, you will need to research a site's existing statistics or research the target audiences if it's a new site.

Optimizing Your Files for the Web

Now that you have two sizes to create a layout, and work with for testing and evaluation in the next chapter, you will need to determine the best image format (gif, jpg, png, or svg) and apply image compression for optimized images for the web.

JPG versus PNG-24

In the brief explanation earlier, JPG and PNG-24 are the best option for detailed photographic images. In my experience, I've yet to find an instance where the PNG-24 (unless there is a need for an Alpha Transparency) was a better option than a JPG now that the `srcset` and `sizes` (discussed later in the chapter) attributes are supported in all modern browsers. However, for the sake of this demo, I'll cover compressing both file types.

Compression

When using compression, there is truly no right or wrong way to do it (I bet you are tired of me writing that)! As a visual designer, you are using your best judgment to determine how much compression can be applied to an image before its visual integrity is affected. As lossy JPG compression is applied, the image starts to become visibly pixelated, gaining noticeable artifacts. What you are objectively looking for is the smallest file size, with the most acceptable amount of artifacting possible. It's good to do this exercise on a high density display. Optimizing your images on a low resolution display will ensure that they most likely look pixelated on high density display, but an image optimized on a high density display will still look good on non-low resolution displays, albeit with a larger file size.

For this demo I'm going to use Adobe Photoshop to demonstrate how to resize and compress an image for web use. Download the source files at https://browsersdevicesfonts.com/05-01-image-optimization.zip and find the file titled "image-optimization.jpg", open it up in Photoshop and resize it to 2560 pixels wide while leaving the "Resample" setting set to "Automatic". Resizing the image prior to opening up the compression dialogue box will put less strain on your computer's processor when working with large file sizes **(Figure 5.1)**.

Once the file has been resized, click on "File" in the menu, then click on "Export", then "Save for Web (Legacy)" in the popup menu. This will open the image compression dialogue screen **(Figure 5.2)**.

Figure 5.1

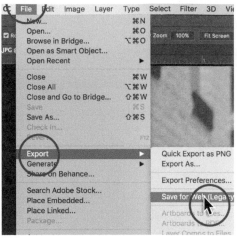

Figure 5.2

Figure 5.3

The "Save for Web" dialogue box defaults to the setting that you last used, so the setting you see on your screen will most likely not match mine, and that's OK. What is important, is that you first select the image format to save your image as. Look for the menu option that will either read "GIF", "JPEG", "PNG-8", or "PNG-24", and select "JPEG" in the dropdown menu **(Figure 5.3)**. Once you've selected the JPEG file format, you will be able to then check the box next to the "Progressive" option. You want your images to load progressively to help preserve your website's layout. By checking "Progressive" you are basically telling the web browser to find the size of the image first and load a low-resolution version as a placeholder until the higher-resolution version is fully loaded. This helps with the layout by telling the web browser that "something is going to go here and is going to be this size" and allow content to flow around the image as it's intended to be placed in your layout. This stops content from jumping around while users are trying to read if they scroll through a page faster than the images can load. This is an oversimplification of the process and is not a magic bullet from a performance perspective, but you should be generally aware of this.

Before you start applying compression, you should also notice that below the image preview window, is a dialogue box where you can change the zoom level of the image. You want to be at a 100% zoom level to fully understand how the compression will affect the image. If you are zoomed out, you won't see the artifacting that is occurring. If you are zoomed in, you will see extra artifacting. You can also click and drag on the image in the preview window to move it around. It's good to focus on areas with large fields of color with subtle color differences like a cloudy sky first. Clouds will tend to get blocky very quickly, showing the artifacts, and will ruin an image sooner than other more detailed areas would.

With the JPEG option selected, there are two different, but related setting options that you can work with. The first option is the dropdown menu with "Low" through "High" settings **(Figure 5.4)**. These are broad settings that change the "Quality" setting in set increments. The second option is the "Quality" dialogue

box where you can enter a numeric value ranging from 0 (lowest quality) to 100 (highest quality). Both of these methods apply lossy compression by removing pixel information. As you adjust the settings you are looking to make the smallest file size possible while not degrading the visual quality of the image too drastically. For this demonstration, I

Figure 5.4

choose to go with a quality of 10, however your tolerance may vary.

While not as effective as running an actual performance test on WebPage Test, there is a utility built into Photoshop that gives you an estimate for how long an image will take to download. I personally like to use the 384 Kbps setting because that replicates a bad 3G cellular connection. Per Photoshop's estimate, it will take 8 seconds for the image to be downloaded, well outside the 3 second threshold users will tolerate when viewing webpages on mobile devices and outside the 1 second threshold for desktop devices. To get it down to an acceptable download time where you aren't going to alienate users, they would need to have a connection running at 2 Mbps, which is within the capabilities of a 4G LTE connection under ideal conditions.

Removing Metadata

Another step you can take to reduce your file sizes is to remove unnecessary metadata. By default, cameras save a lot of information not related to how the image is actually displayed on the screen. For example, a camera will store additional information such as time, date, location, F-stop and ISO settings, and more **(Figure 5.5)**. When you save for web in Photoshop some of the metadata is removed, but not all of it. To get the final bit of unnecessary information out of your .jpg and .png images simply drag and drop your files into ImageOptim **(Figure 5.6)**.

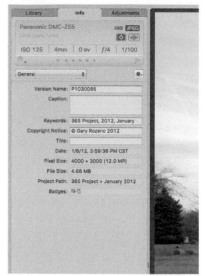

Figure 5.5

Figure 5.6

ImageOptim can also apply lossy compression like you just did in Photoshop. I prefer to have the preview screen that Photoshop supplies, so be sure to disable lossy compression in the ImageOptim preferences **(Figure 5.7)**. ImageO ptim is only available on macOS so if you are running Windows you will need to look into another program such as JPEG & PNG Stripper. Since it only adds a simple drag and drop step to your process it's worth the extra step to finetune your images.

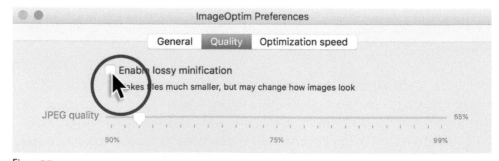

Figure 5.7

PNG versus SVG (and GIF too)

Aside from learning to distinguish how much compression to apply to an image, when I'm working with my students, it's pretty straight forward for them on when to use the JPG format. The real gray area comes when they start trying to incorporate icons and illustrations into their work. With GIF, PNG, and SVG file formats to choose from, students often make the wrong choice, leading to fuzzy bitmapped images, slow loading websites, or worse: front-end developers making design decisions and adjusting your icons and illustrations accordingly.

As already alluded to in the previous section, you want to use the SVG format whenever possible because it supports vector graphics. Since vector images are infinitely scalable, they will render with the best resolution the device is capable of, be it a smartphone with a high-density display, or a 27-inch 5k monitor. Another bonus to SVG images is that they can be styled with CSS. This means that if you are incorporating an icon that will have multiple colors or hover states throughout the visual design, one SVG icon styled with CSS will replace the multiple GIF or PNG icons necessary for the design's color scheme.

Iconography

Between Icons and Illustrations, the former is the most straightforward for my students to understand. When icons are simple shapes, the SVG format can offer significant file savings in addition to adding the flexibility to be styled with CSS and animated. To test if you should be using an SVG instead of a GIF, or PNG, simply compare files sizes!

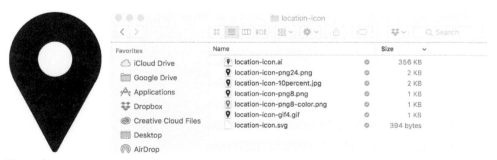

Figure 5.8

As you can see in (Figure 5.8), a location icon saved as a 394 byte SVG is almost one-third the file size of a 1 kilobyte GIF or PNG. If you need multiple colors of the icon for hover and other state changes, it drops to a quarter or less the size of the GIF/PNG icon set which has a fixed height of 200 pixels. Meaning, if the icon were to be upsized, it would become pixelated. However, the location icon isn't the only situation best served using SVG images. SVGs can handle more complex images such as logos. Being able to infinitely scale a logo is much more plausible than scaling a location icon. In **Figure 5.9**, you can see the more complex Design Edu Today logo is still smaller than its GIF and PNG counterparts.

Figure 5.9

Illustrations

When it comes to the use of SVGs versus GIFs or PNGs, saving illustrations is the gray area. The more complex an illustration gets, the more nodes it has, and the larger the file size gets. Adding a few colors and simple rectangular shapes to the Design Edu Today logo in **Figure 5.10** creates a file size 6 times the original. At 19kb the file size is still small enough to consider it for use, especially considering it's infinitely scalable and will look great on high-density (retina) displays. However, take a look at the 851 × 315 pixel "designed-facebook-banner.png" file. It's only 9kb, half the size of the SVG. If you want to ensure that the PNG file will look good on a high-density display, you need to double its size to 1702 × 630 pixels. Because the color pallet in the image doesn't change in the "designed-facebook-banner-x2.png" file—even though it's doubled in size—it's still only 10kb and will look good on high density devices. When in doubt about which file format to use, talk to your front-end developer. There are many more ways to optimize an SVG that are beyond the scope of this book that could make a fairly complex illustration quite small in file size.

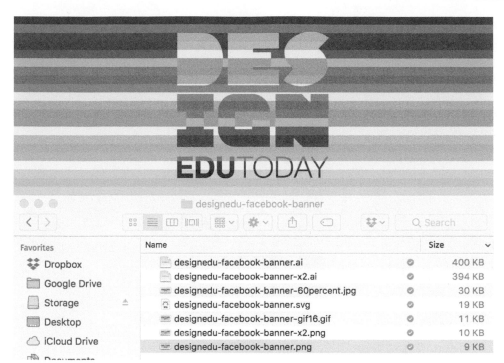

Figure 5.10

Part One: Creating Pages with HTML & CSS for Context

Faux Layouts

Now that you have learned in the previous chapters how to add custom fonts to a web page, and you've just learned how to optimize your images, you can put all of those skills together and create a page with just enough content to accurately evaluate and test your visual design choices for layout and performance. There are many existing HTML and CSS frameworks such as the very popular Bootstrap and Zurb Foundation that could be used to quickly create layouts for evaluation and testing as well. However, these frameworks have a lot of extras built in that would potentially throw off the performance testing. These frameworks tend to predefine the breakpoints for you as well, making it harder for you to identify when the content dictates a change in the column widths of your visual design.

I could also demonstrate how to use the CSS Grid property to create a simple layout for testing, and quite frankly this would be the most accurate method. Unfortunately, there is still a big enough learning curve for CSS Grid that as a Visual Designer, you'd be spending more time developing than designing if you were going to use this approach. Additionally, you truly don't need to see an entire web page to evaluate and test your visual design choices, you just need to see how certain elements of your design behave coded in a browser window across devices. After all, what you are really trying to do is accurately evaluate when the content in your columns gets too skinny to read properly, and test if the combination of fonts and images slows your site down too much.

Using the Layout Evaluation Template

To instruct my own students, I created a simple grid only HTML and CSS template for them to work from. The template lets students create a 12 column based grid layout with real content that can be evaluated to determine everything from optimal reading line lengths to when to change the cropping of an image. The simple layout evaluation template should not be considered best practices when writing HTML and CSS and would make front-end developers cringe if you were to try and use this to produce live webpages for your clients. However, using this template is the easiest way I found to get my graphic designers evaluating their design choices in actual browsers, on multiple devices, in the shortest amount of time possible.

Since there is no difference between using the Browser or Native Application based workflows when it comes to the following demonstration, I'm only showing images on how to do this in CodePen. However, if you are using the Native Application based workflow you will still write the exact same HTML and CSS. When there is a difference in the code I write each specifically.

You will need to have a CodePen Pro subscription to follow along with this demo because you will be uploading assets, including images in this section, and fonts in the next section. If you are using the Native Application based workflow you will already have everything that you need.

Now, to get started for CodePen Pro users, you need to fork the "Layout Evaluation Template" at https://codepen.io/browsersdevicesfonts/pen/RyRbwr **(Figure 5.11)** and either work directly from the newly forked pen or fork it one more time to leave the original in your collection as a template. For those of you working in Brackets download and open the "Layout Evaluation Template" at https:// browsersdevicesfonts.com/exercise-files/05-03-layout-evaluation-template.zip.

Regardless of working method you will need to download the sample images titled "05-02-layout-evaluation-images" from https://codepen.io/browsersdevices-fonts/exercise-files/05-02-layout-evaluation-images.zip

Figure 5.11

While the layout in the following demo will consist of a single hero image followed by a row containing three columns of text, you are not limited to this layout. In fact, you can have any combination of rows and columns based on a 12 column grid that you can imagine. When you scroll through the HTML (editor panel or index.html file) you will notice a pattern of `<div class="row">` surrounding any combination of `<div class="col-">`'s where the sum of the col-'s equals 12. As long as the sum of `<div class="col-">`'s inside of a `<div class="row">` total 12 the template will handle the layout. Remember, while this may seem restricting, the goal of the template is not to build a working web page. The goal of this exercise is to get enough of the content into the browser, so you can make sound visual design choices in your layout program.

CodePen Pro users, upload the 2560 pixel wide image you optimized in the previous section and click on the drop down menu button next to the image once it's uploaded to reveal the menu and select "Copy as <img> tag" **(Figures 5.12 & 5.13)**.

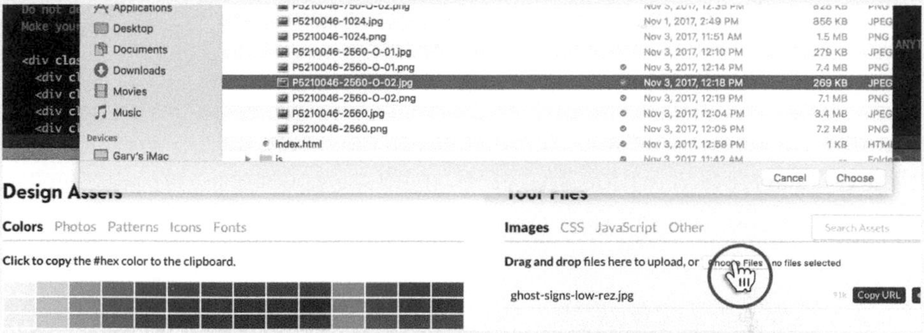

Figure 5.12

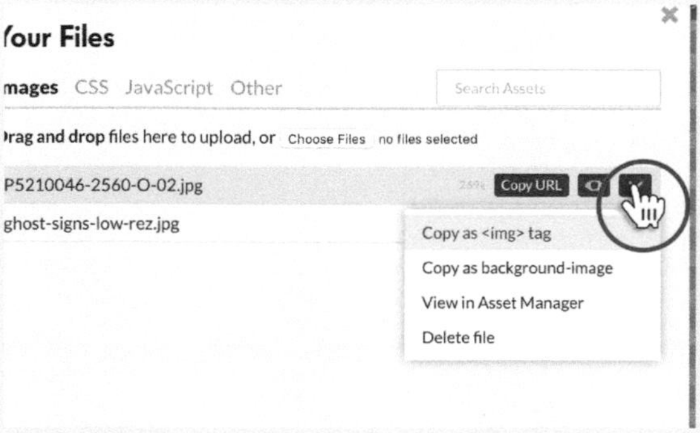

Figure 5.13

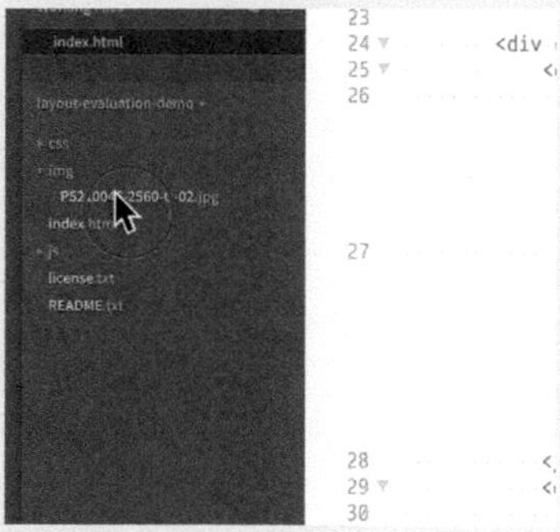

Figure 5.14

Brackets users, copy the 2560 pixel wide image you optimized in the previous section into the "img" folder **(Figure 5.14)**.

Next, clean out the example column combinations that I put in for reference and make your pen match the following **(Figure 5.15)**.

```
<div class="row">
    <div class="col-12"></div>
</div>

<div class="row">
    <div class="col-4"></div>
    <div class="col-4"></div>
    <div class="col-4"></div>
</div>
```

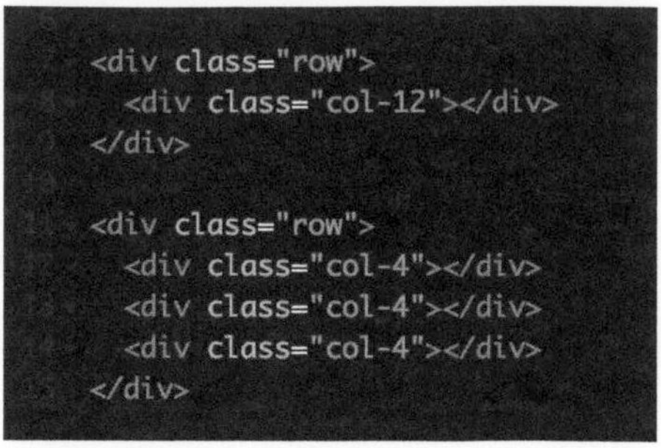

Figure 5.15

Now you can paste the image tag you copied from the asset panel into the HTML editor panel, so your code looks similar to the following (except for a unique URL for the image you uploaded) **(Figures 5.16 & 5.17)**.

Browser Specific Workflow Code

```
<div class="row">
    <div class="col-12"><img src='https://s3-us-west-2.
amazonaws.com/s.cdpn.io/135363/P5210046-2560-0-02.jpg'
alt=''></div>
</div>
```

Figure 5.16

```
<div class="row">
    <div class="col-12"><img src='img/P5210046-2560-O-02.
jpg' alt=''></div>
</div>
```

Figure 5.17

With the updates to the HTML you should now see the image of the cat showing up in the preview panel. Of course, when you are using this process for your client work, it should go without saying that you should be using the images that will be used in the final visual design, not a For Position Only (FPO) image of Snowball, the feral cat I feed in my backyard.

With the image in place, you need to put text into the layout to properly evaluate column widths. You should be using real copy when you are incorporating this process into your own daily workflow because evaluating dummy copy for readability, isn't nearly as effective as the real thing. However, since this is simply an exercise to demonstrate how to build a page for evaluation and testing, I will use text that came from the *Typographic Hierarchy Page*. I'm also using two paragraphs worth of text as well. You can use more, but I suggest using a minimum of two paragraphs in at least one of the columns **(Figure 5.18)**. You will be surprised to see just how much a visual design can change based on how multiple paragraphs of text reflow to fill the unique screen of each user.

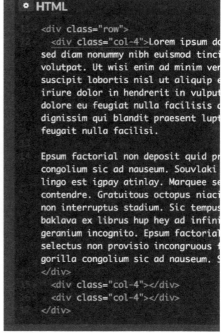

Figure 5.18

Once you have pasted the text into the HTML (editor panel or index.html file), you will need to wrap each individual paragraph in a <p> tag. Since HTML ignores any extra space beyond a single space, the paragraphs will run together into one big paragraph. Be sure to close each paragraph out with a `</p>` tag, or you will inadvertently cause other issues in the faux layout you are creating. When done, yours should look similar to **Figure 5.19**.

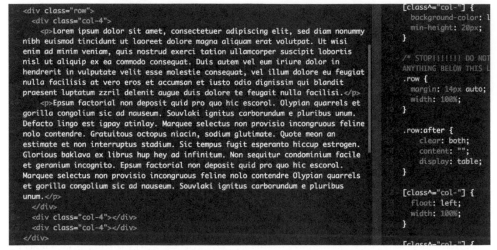

Figure 5.19

Once you've wrapped the initial paragraphs with `<p>` tags, copy and paste that text into the two remaining columns **(Figure 5.20)**.

Figure 5.20

CodePen Pro users, with all the text copied into the layout, click on the "Change View" button and then click on the "Live View" option **(Figure 5.21)**. Please note that the Live View option is only available for the CodePen Pro subscribers.

Brackets users: With the image and copy in place, click on the "Live Preview" icon to immediately have your page open up in Chrome for a quick evaluation. If you haven't already, start Browsersync to fully evaluate the layout with your device lab.

Figure 5.21

Once you are finished, you can change the screen size to view how your faux layout will look at different sizes **(Figures 5.22 & 5.23)**. What you should be looking for as you resize the screen will be discussed in further detail in the next section.

Figure 5.22

Lorem ipsum dolor sit amet, consectetuer adipiscing elit, sed diam nonummy nibh euismod tincidunt ut laoreet dolore magna aliquam erat volutpat. Ut wisi enim ad minim veniam, quis nostrud exerci tation

Lorem ipsum dolor sit amet, consectetuer adipiscing elit, sed diam nonummy nibh euismod tincidunt ut laoreet dolore magna aliquam erat volutpat. Ut wisi enim ad minim veniam, quis nostrud exerci tation

Lorem ipsum dolor sit amet, consectetuer adipiscing elit, sed diam nonummy nibh euismod tincidunt ut laoreet dolore magna aliquam erat volutpat. Ut wisi enim ad minim veniam, quis nostrud exerci tation

Figure 5.23

What's Next?

Now that you have content in a browser window on actual devices, there are a lot of visual design choices that will have to be made. Everything from determining the optimal line reading length for body copy, when to change the cropping of an image, to when to reduce the number of columns in your designs. Making these evaluations early on in the visual design process will prevent a lot of costly back and forth revision between you and your front-end developer.

Part Two: Evaluating HTML &
CSS Pages with Context

First, before you get started in this section, complete the demos in the previous section and have the sample layout ready as you begin. It's much easier to do all the necessary evaluations and performance testing if you have a sample layout in front of you.

As demonstrated in previous chapters, just because you are designing on a screen for a screen, scale is still a major issue. It never ceases to amaze me how students ignore my advice to look at things in actual scale before they get too far into their visual designs. What usually ends up happening is they will spend a lot of time on a desktop sized layout that fits neatly into their screen going into a lot of exacting detail, only to realize that their column widths are either too big, too small, or non-existent, failing to support the content on other devices. This realization means that the student would either have to give the front-end developer (if this were client work) layouts that were inaccurate and leave critical visual design decisions up to the developer or start the design process over. If the students haven't gotten too far in the visual design process, starting over isn't that big of a deal. If they've done a lot of work, starting over with the correct scale can put them days, if not weeks behind.

Had the students gone straight from wireframe to the faux layout demonstrated in Part One of this chapter, they'd know exactly the scale necessary for their layouts before they started the visual design process in a program like Sketch or Xd. In this section, I'm going to demonstrate how to evaluate your faux layouts to start the visual design process off on the right foot.

Where Does This Fit into Your Design Process?

As we all know, students resist sketching out their ideas at first and prefer to jump straight into the computer. It's undisputed that sketching your ideas first saves time in the long run, especially with web design layouts. However, instead of being the old guy yelling at the kids to "Get off my lawn!", I've spent a lot of time working with students to understand why they don't work on paper first. Their reluctance has to do with not understanding our old nemesis, scale. Students will jump right into Sketch or Xd and start pasting in all their content on the desktop layout that first comes to mind. The layout may look good on their screen, but they haven't stopped to take into consideration mobile first, progressive enhancement or responsive design principles. They just assume that their visual design choices will work on all devices. Once I challenge them to look at their design on an actual device, they realize it is way off and will either stubbornly plow forward with an inconsistent, untenable visual layout, or go back to the drawing board.

So why did I just make you read that preamble? It's important to remind you that we are not making extensive visual design choices at this stage with our faux layouts. This stage of the visual design process is meant to quickly make and test *blueprints* of the potential layout of a webpage. All you are looking to do is determine if your layout's grid works as expected, and then determine when the layout's grid needs to change to continue to support optimal readability for the user based on actual content.

So where does this stage fit in the visual design process then? Simple, after you have created a Style Tile or Mood Board and made your font choices, but before you begin pasting content into your layout program. Once you have some of the actual content from your client, break out your sketchbook and start to wireframe. However, don't make the same mistake those new to the interactive design process make by confusing wireframes with thumbnails or sketches. For the sake of this exercise, wireframes are literally design agnostic rectangles and squares that represent the physical location of a web page's content.

Too often wireframes start to take on the eventual visual appearance of a website by fully flushing out details like iconography, navigation menus, etc. That's not what wireframes are meant for. That's why I prefer sketchbooks with a faint dot grid pattern versus full gridded or plain paged sketchbook for this part of the process **(Figure 5.24)**. At least for me, the gridded sketchbook makes this process feel less like visual design since wireframes are meant to be quick studies of where to place content on a page, not what the page will visually look like.

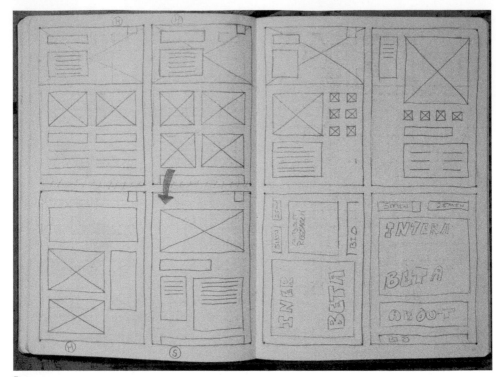

Figure 5.24

This is where the students' frustration with sketching comes in. Why should they sketch out font pairs, color palettes, or buttons when they can experiment with making those visual design choices in a layout program quickly and accurately? Once I demonstrate my expectations for creating multiple wireframes in a sketchbook, students are more receptive to the process. This also saves me from having to yell "Get off my lawn!" in my grumpy old man voice.

Armed with a few pages of wireframe concepts sketched out in your notebook—based on actual content supplied by the client—you can start to make your own faux layout pages using the process and template described in the previous section. You want to do this before you start working on your static mockups in Sketch or Xd. It's also good to have the *Font Specimen Page*, and the *Typographic Hierarchy Page* exercises completed before you start the faux layout process. Since you will be evaluating the faux layout for readability and performance among other things, your typographic choices are important for proper testing.

The Layout Choices You Actually Need to Evaluate and Test

Evaluating Optimal Line Lengths in Layouts

As discussed in Chapter 04 *Typography* and throughout this book, there is a lot of reading done online with a lot of studies to back that claim up. Since there is so much reading done online, designing layouts, specifically breakpoints,[1] that are based on the readability of text is an excellent way to approach responsive web design. There are a lot of good books on the specifics of typography and web typography such as *Typographic Web Design* by Laura Franz, and The *New Web Typography* by Stephen Boss and Jason Cranford Teague and most of those resources agree that the optimal reading length of a line of text on a screen is between 45 and 75 characters per line. Of course, those are the extremes and will vary based on the width and x-height of a specific font, but it's a good range to start within. Since you know the optimal character range for reading, and you know either the necessary font size or the necessary column width, you can easily base your layouts on ideal reading conditions.

Turning on the Character Counter

To save my own students the hassle of having to count the character range manually, I've developed a handy tool in the *Layout Evaluation Template*, so they can easily identify if their typographic choices within a layout are optimal for the reader. Since there is no difference between using the Browser or Native Application based workflows when it comes to the following demonstration, I'm only showing images on how to do this in CodePen. However, if you are using the Native Application based workflow you will still write the exact same HTML and CSS.

---

1   W3 Schools. 2018. How TO - Typical Device Breakpoints. https://www.w3schools.com/howto/howto_css_media_query_breakpoints.asp (accessed April 29, 2018).

To use the Character Counter, open the faux layout you created in the previous section using either the Browser or Native Application based workflow. Within the HTML panel, or index.html file look for a block of copy marked up with a `<p></p>` tag **(Figure 5.25)**. Next, update the leading `<p>` tag with an ID so it looks like `<p id="characters">` seen in **Figure 5.26** and leave the closing `</p>` tag in place without any changes. This will enable the Character Counter to highlight all the characters within the `<p id="characters"></p>` tag in the 45–75 character range in yellow.

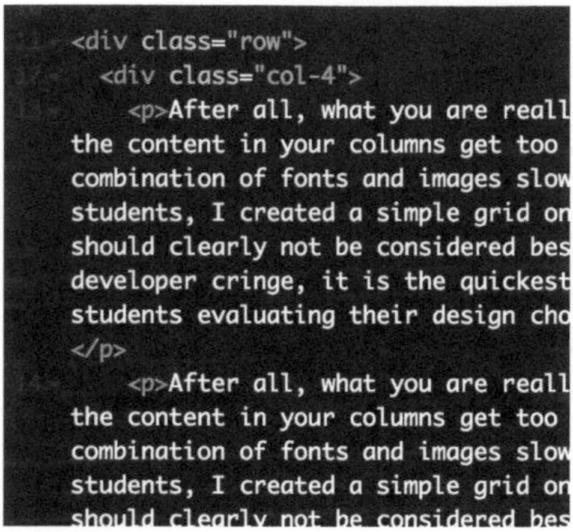

Figure 5.25

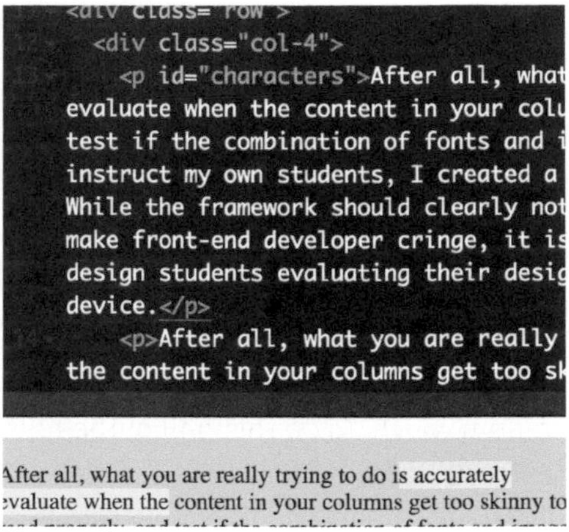

Figure 5.26

With the character count highlighted, you can see that with the default font size of 16 pixels and a 3 column layout in a viewport (open browser window) of 1280 pixels is close to optimal. The line length is breaking somewhere in the middle of the 45–75 character range. This is probably a good balance between font size and line length for a callout or synopsis of a longer article on a website's homepage. For a long form article, it would probably be a little difficult to read after a while, and you would want a wider column such as in **Figure 5.26**.

To continue to evaluate and test your layouts for optimal reading length, delete the third column of text, basically everything between and including the

```
<div class="col-4">
    <p></p>
</div>
```

HTML tags. Once you have deleted the third column, change the `class="col-4"` in the remaining two columns from `class="col-4"` to `class="col-6"`. This will change your faux layout to two columns spanning the 12 column grid **(Figure 5.27)**.

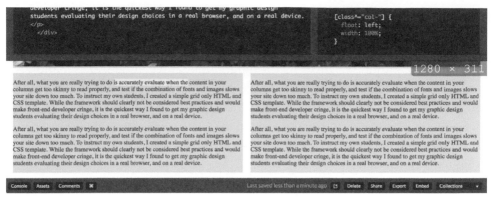

Figure 5.27

Unfortunately, this change from three columns to two columns with a 1280 pixel wide viewport and 16 pixel default font size creates a poor reading experience for the user. The text size is too small, creating longer line lengths that will not be optimal for long form reading. To compensate for this, you could change your column width, but you'd be back to the same issue you were facing previously. In this instance, it would be better to make the font size bigger to properly fill the column width. To do this, adjust the font size to 20 pixels by adding the following to the CSS editor panel, or styles.css file depending on your working method.

```
body {
    font-size: 20px;
}
```

Figure 5.28

Once you make this adjustment, you will see the optimal line length for long form reading has been achieved for a 2 column layout on a twelve column grid in a 1280 pixel wide viewport with a 20 pixel font size **(Figure 5.29)**. However, you will notice in this demonstration, we are using the default font as well. CodePen is loading a sans-serif and Brackets is most likely loading a serif. Since these aren't the fonts you will be using, add in your own font choice using either the @font-face, Google Fonts, or Typekit method demonstrated in Chapter 04 *Typography*.

In **Figure 5.29**, you can see that I've added Open Sans Pro from Google Fonts which is a slightly wider font than the default sans-serif that was being used in **Figure 5.28**. I ended up going with a font size of 21 pixels and increased the line height to 1.4 to make it a bit easier to read **(Figure 5.30)**. You will adjust these settings to suit the font you chose for your visual designs.

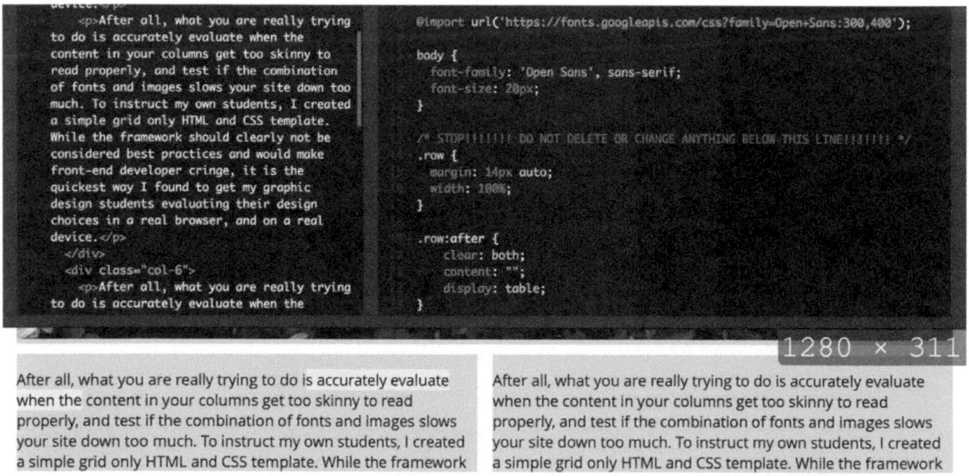

Figure 5.29

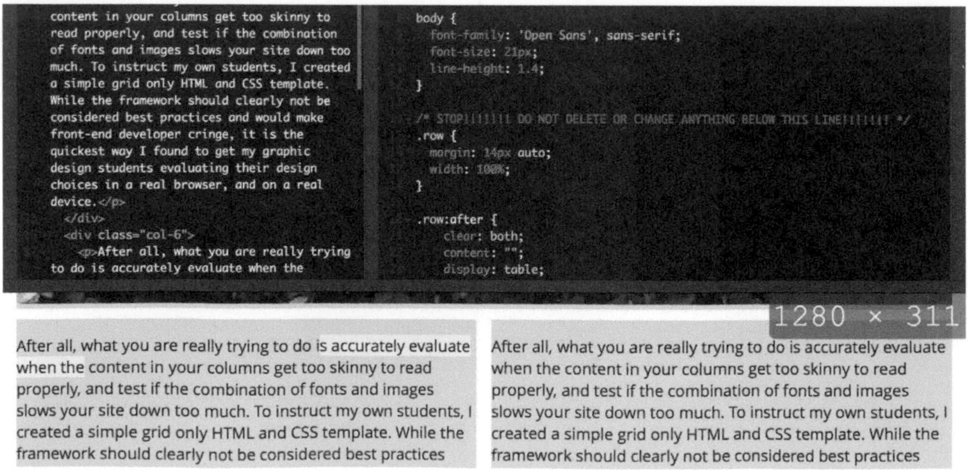

Figure 5.30

Armed with the knowledge of your viewport width (in this case 1280 pixels) and font size (21 pixels) you are now ready to start setting up your project in something like Sketch or Xd **(Figure 5.31)**. In your layout program, you will want to start by simply creating an artboard with a width of 1280 pixels (or whatever dimension matches what you have in your faux layout template). Next, you should set up whatever number of columns you have on a twelve-unit grid and place your text in the layout and choose the font size and line height that matches what you determined from the faux layout.

ccurately
get too skinny

Figure 5.31

However, you are not done with the evaluation process yet. Remember, the web is responsive! Your website is not going to only be viewed on a 1280 pixel wide device. It could be viewed on everything from an iPhone 4s to a 42" TV via a Sony PlayStation. The optimal line reading length will obviously change based on the width of the device **(Figures 5.32 & 5.33)**.

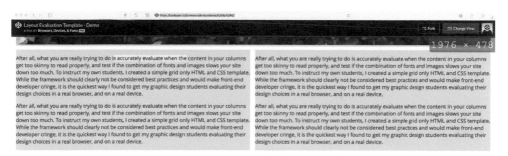

Figure 5.32

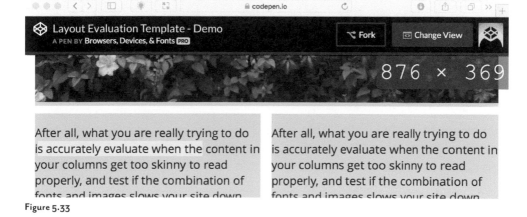

Figure 5.33

It's at precisely this point where visual designers distinguish themselves from their peers. You can make the choice to jump straight into making your mockups, or you can determine multiple optimal line lengths and pass along that information to your front-end developer. In the next section you will learn how to evaluate, test, and create CSS instructions for your faux layouts to determine breakpoints for adjusting your typographic choices for optimal readability.

Determining Breakpoints

Before I dive into how you make visual design decisions based on breakpoints using CSS Media Queries, it's necessary to briefly discuss their history. Prior to the release of the original iPhone in 2007 websites were a fixed width of 960 pixel wide layout that was centered in the browser window on a screen generally 1024 pixels wide. Around the time of the release of the iPhone, savvy designers and developers were making two different sized websites: one fixed width for desktop and one fluid single column width for mobile. Quickly realizing that this solution was untenable, new features were added to the HTML and CSS specifications. These new features gave web browsers the ability to detect the width of the open browsers window (viewport) and deliver instructions on how to visually style specific elements based on the width of the open viewport. However, it wasn't until May 25th, 2010, that these new features for the HTML and CSS specifications were formalized into a process by Ethan Marcotte in his seminal "Responsive Web Design"[2] article on the *A List Apart* blog.

For the new Responsive Design process to work, two things need to happen. First, the new HTML meta tag properties viewport and width need to be added to each HTML file between the `<head></head>` tags like so `<meta name="viewport" content="width=device-width, initial-scale=1">`. I've already supplied this meta tag to the Native Application templates and CodePen automatically adds them behind the scenes. Adding the meta tag property viewport allows the web browser to detect the size of the viewport in real time. Meaning, if you resize the viewport, the web browser is constantly calculating and updating the size.

The second thing that needs to happen is the web browser needs to know how to style an element via CSS based on the size of the open viewport. Fortunately, this ability was added to the CSS specification via the `@media` rule. The `@media`

---

2   Marcotte, Ethan. 2010. Responsive Web Design. https://alistapart.com/article/responsive-web-design/ (accessed April 27, 2018).

rule lets you define what something looks like based on a viewport's dimensions if that size meets a set of predefined conditions. In the following example of a media query, the CSS rule targets devices with screen resolutions 640 pixels or smaller.

```
@media screen and (max-device-width: 640px) {…}
```

The options (declarations) available as part of the @media rule to target devices are nearly limitless. In the following example, the media query targets devices that are between 1200 and 1600 pixels with a high-density display.

```
@media screen
    and (min-device-width: 1200px)
    and (max-device-width: 1600px)
    and (-webkit-min-device-pixel-ratio: 2)
    and (min-resolution: 192dpi) {…}
```

Full disclosure, as a Visual Designer, you don't need to know all the possible options for targeting devices with media queries. In fact, you should not be targeting devices at all. Instead, you need to target the point when content becomes difficult for the user to read. To that end, as Visual Designers, you can get away with utilizing a simplified version of the media query that targets a viewport's width in the following ways @media screen and (min-width: 600px) {…} and @media screen and (max-width: 1024px) {…}.

Adding Media Queries

As previously mentioned, a single set of typographic choices in a layout for one screen size is not going to work across a multitude of devices. Fortunately, it's pretty easy—thanks to media queries— to give the browser multiple sets of instructions on how to visually style your content. Picking up where we left off in the evaluation and testing process you will notice the typographic choices for a 1280 pixel wide viewport **(Figure 5.34)**, but what happens when that viewport is wider than 1280 pixels? As you'll see in **(Figure 5.35)**, the layout no longer has an optimal line length for long form reading.

Figure 5.34

Figure 5.35

There are two ways to solve this problem. You could switch to a 3 column layout at 1624 pixels wide and leave the font size alone **(Figure 5.36)**.

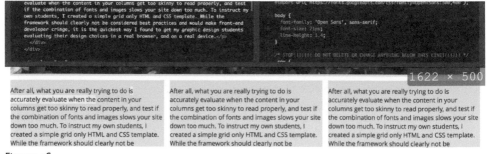

Figure 5.36

You could also approach this visual design problem by giving the browser instructions to increase the font size when the viewport is 1624 pixels wide or wider **(Figure 5.36)**. To do this, you need to add a `@media screen and (min-width: 1624px) {...}` declaration to either the CSS editor panel or your styles.css file. This media query tells the browser that if the viewport is 1624 pixels wide, or wider do something. Your something will be to change the font size of the body element by adding the following CSS.

```
@media screen and (min-width: 1624px) {
    body {
        font-family: 'Open Sans', sans-serif;
        font-size: 26px;
        line-height: 1.4;
    }
}
```

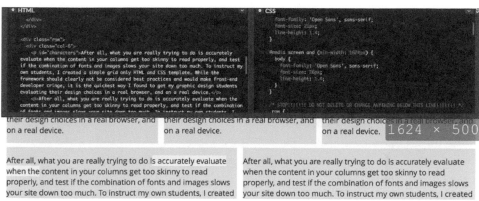

Figure 5.37

As you can see changing the font size from 21 to 26 pixels brought the optimal line length back to where it needs to be for our 2 column, 1624 pixel wide layout **(Figure 5.37)**. Regardless if you choose to use a 3 column layout or increase the font size to get your text at optimal line reading length, this becomes a breakpoint in your layout. Armed with this information, you should go back into your layout program of choice and create a new 1624 pixel wide artboard that represents the visual design decisions you made in this exercise **(Figures 5.38 & 5.39)**.

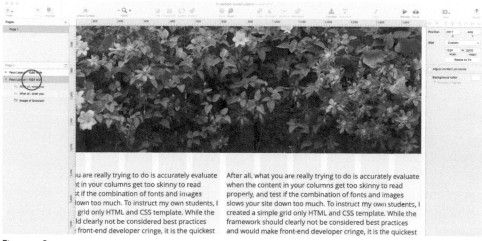

Figure 5.38

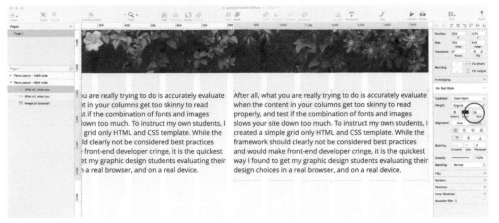

Figure 5.39

But wait! You aren't done testing and evaluating yet. You still need to plan out what you are going to do for larger edge cases such as 21", 24", and 27" displays. When you increase the viewport to 2020 pixels wide, the optimal reading length breaks down again. To get the layout back to the optimal line length, again you can go to a 3 column layout or add another media query for the body font size by adding the following CSS **(Figure 5.40)**.

```
@media screen and (min-width: 2020px) {
    body {
        font-size: 30px;
    }
}
```

Notice that I removed both the `font-family` and `line-height`. Since they were already defined once and haven't changed, we don't need to repeat them. At this point, you can create another artboard in your layout program that is 2020 pixels wide and displays the revised visual design choices.

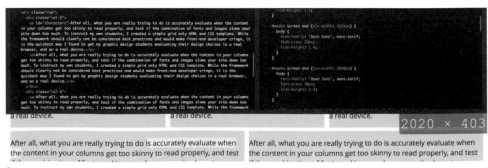

Figure 5.40

Before going any further, it is a good time to interject with a reminder that I'm demonstrating a quick evaluation method using CSS for graphic designers. This method would not be considered best practice for production code written by a front-end developer. While graphic designers tend to work large (desktop) to small (phone), front-end developers work in the opposite direction. For example, a front-end developer would most likely never write the media rule `@media screen and (max-width: 863px) {…}` that only targets viewports smaller than 863 pixels. Instead they would use a mobile first approach where all the code they write specifically targets small devices, the dominant way web content is consumed. Once the code is written for the smaller devices, the front-end developer will use media rules such as `@media screen and (min-width: 863px) {…}` or `@media screen and (min-width: 1280px) {…}` to progressively enhance the experience for tablet, laptop, and desktop users by overwriting previous CSS declarations.

It's also important to note that a front-end developer's decision to work from small to large is not arbitrary. By writing CSS that targets small devices first, then adding select rules that overwrite specific design decisions based on viewport size is much more efficient for myriad reasons. Perhaps the biggest reason is this approach ensures that users with older devices and browsers will still be able to view and use the website, while users with newer devices and modern browsers get an enhanced experience. I suggest that as a graphic designer, you also try and work from small to large when you start the design process on your next project.

Ok, now that you've found breakpoints for medium and large sized screens, what about smaller sized screens? Yes, you need to check test and evaluate them too! For example, once the viewport decreases to less than 863 pixels wide the optimal line length needs adjusting, and a new breakpoint needs to be added **(Figure 5.41)**. In this case, you need to use a different media query, one that targets a specific size and anything smaller than that.

```
@media screen and (max-width: 863px) {
    body {
        font-size: 16px;
        line-height: 1.3;
    }
}
```

Notice I also changed the line height. At the smaller size, there was too much line height, so I reduced it. If you've noticed a pattern where I state, "Now make an artboard in your layout program," that's good, but also bad. I made the following adjustment based on what the layout looked like on my 27" retina iMac. I need to look at the layout on actual devices first, to determine if my visual design choices truly work.

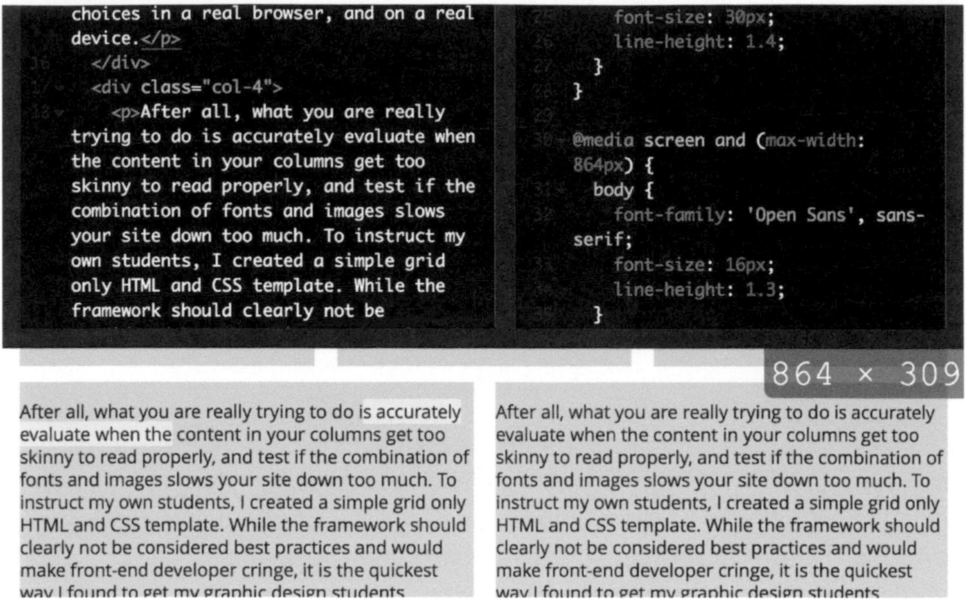

```
choices in a real browser, and on a real
device.</p>
  </div>
  <div class="col-4">
    <p>After all, what you are really
trying to do is accurately evaluate when
the content in your columns get too
skinny to read properly, and test if the
combination of fonts and images slows
your site down too much. To instruct my
own students, I created a simple grid
only HTML and CSS template. While the
framework should clearly not be
```

```
      font-size: 30px;
      line-height: 1.4;
    }
}

@media screen and (max-width:
864px) {
  body {
    font-family: 'Open Sans', sans-
serif;
    font-size: 16px;
    line-height: 1.3;
  }
```

864 × 309

After all, what you are really trying to do is accurately evaluate when the content in your columns get too skinny to read properly, and test if the combination of fonts and images slows your site down too much. To instruct my own students, I created a simple grid only HTML and CSS template. While the framework should clearly not be considered best practices and would make front-end developer cringe, it is the quickest way I found to get my graphic design students

After all, what you are really trying to do is accurately evaluate when the content in your columns get too skinny to read properly, and test if the combination of fonts and images slows your site down too much. To instruct my own students, I created a simple grid only HTML and CSS template. While the framework should clearly not be considered best practices and would make front-end developer cringe, it is the quickest way I found to get my graphic design students

Figure 5.41

I know from experience that a two column layout is not going to work for long form reading on smaller devices, so I added a single column that spanned all twelve units of the grid **(Figure 5.42)**. Obviously, the single column isn't going to work at 1280 pixels wide. However, let's take a look at that layout on an actual device from your device lab.

1280 × 465

After all, what you are really trying to do is accurately evaluate when the content in your columns get too skinny to read properly, and test if the combination of fonts and images slows your site down too much. To instruct my own students, I created a simple grid only HTML and CSS template. While the framework should clearly not be considered best practices and would make front-end developer cringe, it is the quickest way I found to get my graphic design students evaluating their design choices in a real browser, and on a real device.

After all, what you are really trying to do is accurately evaluate when the content in your columns get too skinny to read

After all, what you are really trying to do is accurately evaluate when the content in your columns get too skinny to read

After all, what you are really trying to do is accurately evaluate when the content in your columns get too skinny to read

Figure 5.42

You can see what the layout looks like on an iPhone 7 plus **(Figure 5.43)**. Most likely in the printed version of the screenshot you won't really be able to tell, but if you are looking at this on an actual device, you will notice that the font size of 16 pixels is too small for comfortable long form reading.

After adjusting the font size a few times, I finally arrived at an ideal font size of 20 pixels with a line height of 1.35 **(Figure 5.44)**. This is where you can make a new artboard in your layout program that follows along with the visual design choices you just made.

414 × 2202

After all, what you are really trying to do is accurately evaluate when the content in your columns get too skinny to read properly, and test if the combination of fonts and images slows your site down too much. To instruct my own students, I created a simple grid only HTML and CSS template. While the framework should clearly not be considered best practices and would make front-end developer cringe, it is the quickest way I found to get my graphic design students evaluating their design choices in a real browser, and on a real device.

Figure 5.43

```
@media screen and (max-
width: 863px) {
    body {
        font-size: 20px;
        line-height: 1.35;
    }
}
```

For the fun of it, resize your viewport window on your desktop devices as close as you can to the width of the layout on your mobile device. It's amazing how different the scale between the two different devices is. **Figure 5.44** and **Figure 5.45** are the exact same layout and font size, but the screenshot for **Figure 5.44** was taken on an iPhone 7 Plus and the screenshot for **Figure 5.45** was taken on my 27" iMac. The font size in **Figure 5.45** looks huge on my iMac yet is perfect for long form reading on my Android device.

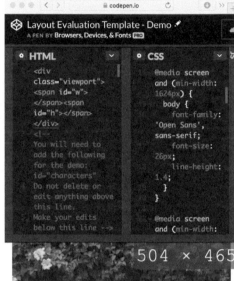

Figure 5.44

Figure 5.45

You can continue to resize the viewport looking for when your content becomes too difficult to determine the necessary breakpoints. But this is a lot of work, and you will end up with a lot of artboards in your layout program so read the last chapter to find out what you really need to hand off to the developer **(Figure 5.46)**. It's not as much as you think!

Figure 5.46

Remember, if you don't make these visual design decisions, they will be made for you by someone who may not have the visual design training and experience that you do.

Evaluating Images in Layouts

Building off the lessons in the previous chapters, images are drastically affected by a change in scale just like your typographic choices. The good news about the ever-changing scale images will be placed in is there are many strategies that a visual designer can employ to ensure images deliver the proper message across all devices. Even better news, all of these strategies are easy to test and evaluate in your workflow, and to implement through minimal HTML and CSS.

Art Direction with the Picture Element

The <picture> element is a recent addition to the HTML specification. There are already a lot of good write-ups about the <picture> element so I won't go into much detail about its history. For the sake of this evaluation, think of the `<picture>` element as an Art Director at a photoshoot. As screens change size, an image with a wide point of view will work great on a desktop computer with a wide monitor. However, that same wide point of view image on a mobile device will be difficult to see at the same level of detail. To account for this, the `<picture>` element lets you art direct what image should be viewed on a specific screen size. For example, look at **Figure 5.47**. The way this image is cropped will work well on devices with large, wide screens. However, when viewed on a narrower screen, a lot of detail in the marble statue of the young girl will be lost.

Now, if you look at the picture of the marble statue of the young girl in **Figure 5.48**, the image is zoomed in. This crop, or art direction, of the image is better suited for smaller screens in a portrait orientation. Yet, this image is obviously not suited for larger, wider screens.

Figure 5.47

This is where the `<picture>` element comes into play. You can choose the most appropriate cropping of an image for a specific viewport width using the `<picture>` element to art direct the browser.

To use the `<picture>` element you simply give the web browser a set of instructions via HTML on when to use a specific cropping of an image. In the following HTML example there are three different

Figure 5.48

versions of the image discussed in the example above. Pay particular attention to the information within the `media=" ()"` property. The web browser reads the `media=" ()"` property and displays the image that best fits the current size of the browser window or viewport.

```
<div class="row">
  <div class="col-12">
    <img src="https://s3-us-west-2.amazonaws.com/s.cdpn.io/135363/picture-element-large-lowrez.jpg">
  </div>
</div>
<div class="row">
  <div class="col-12">
    <picture>
      <img src="https://s3-us-west-2.amazonaws.com/s.cdpn.io/135363/picture-element-large-lowrez.jpg">
    </picture>
  </div>
</div>
```

Figure 5.49

To follow along with this demo, fork the Layout Evaluation – Picture Element pen at https://codepen.io/browsersdevicesfonts/pen/ZoOmbd or download the sample files at https:// browsersdevicesfonts.com/exercise-files/05-04-layout-evaluation-picture-element-demo.zip. Again, whichever workflow method you are using, the HTML and CSS is the same. If you are working in Brackets simply make sure your HTML and CSS match what you see in the CodePen screenshots except for the `<img src="…">` URLs. When those are different, I will note the difference.

Once you have the necessary assets ready, take a look at the HTML in **Figure 5.49**. Here you will see that two identical images are being loaded into the layout template. One image is loaded via the `<img>` tag, the other via the `<picture>` tag. Using the "ChangeView" feature in CodePen lets you change it to "LiveView" if you have a Pro subscription. As you can see in **Figure 5.50**, it's easier to see the two identical images on top of each other for evaluation purposes.

Figure 5.50

Now that I can see both images in the browser window, I started to resize the viewport. Putting on my Art Director's hat, as I watched the viewport resize down to 1000 pixels wide, I felt that the focus of the photo was changing from the memorial of the girl, to being more focused on the cemetery in general.

To put the viewer's focus of the image back to the memorial of the girl I made some changes to the contents of the `<picture>` element tag in my HTML that added a breakpoint telling the browser when to change the cropping of the image, and I changed the default image that is initially being loaded by the browser.

Browser Specific Workflow Code

```
<picture>
    <source media="(min-width: 1000px)" srcset="https://
s3-us-west-2.amazonaws.com/s.cdpn.io/135363/picture-ele-
ment-large-lowrez.jpg">
    <img src="https://s3-us-west-2.amazonaws.com/s.cdpn.
io/135363/picture-element-medium-lowrez.jpg">
</picture>
```

Native Application Specific Workflow Code

```
<picture>
    <source media="(min-width: 1000px)" srcset="img/pic-
ture-element-large-lowrez.jpg">
    <img src="img/picture-element-medium-lowrez.jpg">
</picture>
```

By adding the `<source media="()" srcset="">` to the ‹picture› tag in my HTML, I'm giving the browser instructions that if the "media" or viewport is a specific size, deliver a predefined image. You can see the results in **Figure 5.51** where the bottom image being art directed with the ‹picture› element changes to an image with a more zoomed crop focusing on the memorial of the little girl. What's actually happening is the web browser is loading the zoomed in crop by default, then changing to the wide angle shot when the browser has a min-width: 1000px.

Figure 5.51

However, I'm not done with my evaluations of the image yet. I've tested the image on large and medium sized devices but haven't tested my image on small devices. As I downsize the open browser window, I started to notice that around 640 pixels wide the details of the memorial began to become harder and harder to distinguish the smaller the viewport got. To compensate for this, I gave the web browser additional information to accurately art direct the image for smaller devices. Specifically, I added another ‹source› to the `<picture>` tag that told the browser to load an image zoomed way into the memorial of the girl **(Figure 5.52)**.

```
<source media="(max-width: 659px)" srcset="https://s3-
us-west-2.amazonaws.com/s.cdpn.io/135363/picture-ele-
ment-small-lowrez.jpg">
```

```
<source media="(max-width: 659px)" srcset="img/pic-
ture-element-small-lowrez.jpg">
```

Figure 5.52

As you can see demonstrated in **Figure 5.52** the final HTML in **Figure 5.53** delivers the optimal art directed cropping of the image for a given viewport width.

```
HTML
  <div class="row">
    <div class="col-12">
      <img src="https://s3-us-west-2.amazonaws.com/s.cdpn.io/135363/picture-element-large-lowrez.jpg">
    </div>
  </div>
  <div class="row">
    <div class="col-12">
      <picture>
        <source media="(min-width: 1000px)"
                srcset="https://s3-us-west-2.amazonaws.com/s.cdpn.io/135363/picture-element-large-lowrez.jpg">
        <source media="(max-width: 659px)"
                srcset="https://s3-us-west-2.amazonaws.com/s.cdpn.io/135363/picture-element-small-lowrez.jpg">
        <img src="https://s3-us-west-2.amazonaws.com/s.cdpn.io/135363/picture-element-medium-lowrez.jpg">
      </picture>
    </div>
  </div>
```

Figure 5.53

You don't have to stick to the single, full screen hero image layout I used in the demonstration. You can insert your own images into the faux layout template using any combination of the 12 column grid. As you can see the large image loses its focus on the memorial in the same sized viewport as the original when it's using 8 of the 12 columns in the grid **(Figure 5.54)**. To compensate for this, the medium sized crop is used in the layout **(Figure 5.55)**.

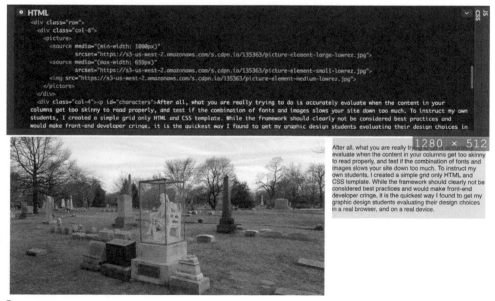

Figure 5.54

```
● HTML                                                                              ∨ 멇
  <div class="row">
    <div class="col-8">
      <picture>
        <source media="(min-width: 659px)"
          srcset="https://s3-us-west-2.amazonaws.com/s.cdpn.io/135363/picture-element-medium-lowrez.jpg">
        <img src="https://s3-us-west-2.amazonaws.com/s.cdpn.io/135363/picture-element-small-lowrez.jpg">
      </picture>
    </div>
    <div class="col-4"><p id="characters">After all, what you are really trying to do is accurately evaluate when the content in your
columns get too skinny to read properly, and test if the combination of fonts and images slows your site down too much. To instruct my own
students, I created a simple grid only HTML and CSS template. While the framework should clearly not be considered best practices and
would make front-end developer cringe, it is the quickest way I found to get my graphic design students evaluating their design choices in
a real browser, and on a real device.</p></div>
  </div>
```

1280 × 512

After all, what you are really trying to do is accurately evaluate when the content in your columns get too skinny to read properly, and test if the combination of fonts and images slows your site down too much. To instruct my own students, I created a simple grid only HTML and CSS template. While the framework should clearly not be considered best practices and would make front-end developer cringe, it is the quickest way I found to get my graphic design students evaluating their design choices in a real browser, and on a real device.

Figure 5.55

Unfortunately, there is no exact science for choosing when to art direct the cropping of an image. The way that seems to work best for my students is starting at either extreme by inserting an image cropped for small screened devices or one cropped for large screens in the Layout Evaluation Template. Once you get an image embedded simply start resizing the screen and evaluate when important details in the larger images start to get lost, or the smaller images get blown up and awkwardly zoomed in filling the screen.

When you find a size where the image would be better served in a different cropping, note the viewport pixel dimensions in the counter and either add another `<source media="()">` inside the `<picture>` element or create a new artboard in your layout program of choice that will demonstrate to the front-end developer where the art direction of the page will need to be changed. I will cover more about preparing your visual design choices for a front-end developer in the final chapter.

Responsive Layouts with Image Grids

Another area of design in which scale will wreak havoc on your layouts is with galleries of images on a grid. If you have never written the HTML and CSS for a responsive website that utilized a grid of images you will most likely approach this design challenge as you would a printed product catalog. In both the print and web layouts you will have a predefined grid to help maintain consistency across multiple pages in a catalog. The print designer will create a single grid and assume that the grid system works on all devices ranging in size from desktop computers all the way down to smartphones. However, this is a dangerous assumption. A layout will simply not appear the same on a larger device **(Figure 5.56)** as it will on a smaller device **(Figure 5.58)**.

The difficulty for print designers new to web design is how do you know when your layout's grid structure is going to break and need to rearrange the layout? With the current crop of prototyping software there is no easy way to resize your artboards in a manner that mimics the content flow of resizing an open web browser window. There also isn't a perfect way to replicate what live code looks like in a browser on a mobile device from your layout program.

Fortunately, as previously demonstrated with typography and the <picture> element, it is pretty easy to get just enough of your visual design choices into the browser to test them on real devices. Better yet, you can do all of this before you begin the visual design process armed only with wireframe sketches, sample content, and the layout evaluation template I've provided you. Adding this process to your work flow will let you spend more time in the visual design process confident that your visual designs will behave as expected in the browser when they are live code.

Determining Breakpoints

Just like determining when to insert a breakpoint for optimal line length for read-ability, the same process applies to images in your grids. In **Figure 5.56** you can see a main product image with alternative product view series of thumbnails to the right and a list of accessories items below. With a viewport of 1280 pixels wide or wider, it's easy to see the details in the smaller thumbnail images. Unfortunately, as the viewport gets smaller and smaller, the thumbnail images get smaller, making it harder to see the original details. By the time you get to a viewport width of 835 pixels wide, the test layout breaks down, making the thumbnail images hard to view in minute details in **Figure 5.57**.

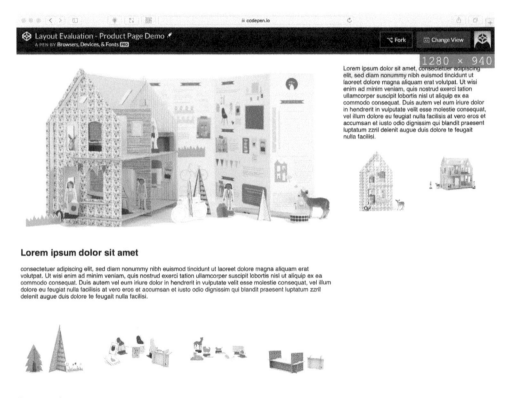

Figure 5.56

835 × 940

Lorem ipsum dolor sit amet, consectetuer adipiscing elit, sed diam nonummy nibh euismod tincidunt ut laoreet dolore magna aliquam erat volutpat. Ut wisi enim ad minim veniam, quis nostrud exerci tation ullamcorper suscipit lobortis nisl ut aliquip ex ea commodo consequat. Duis autem vel eum iriure dolor in hendrerit in vulputate velit esse molestie consequat, vel illum dolore eu feugiat nulla facilisis at vero eros et accumsan et iusto odio dignissim qui blandit praesent luptatum zzril delenit augue duis dolore te feugait nulla facilisi.

Lorem ipsum dolor sit amet

consectetuer adipiscing elit, sed diam nonummy nibh euismod tincidunt ut laoreet dolore magna aliquam erat volutpat. Ut wisi enim ad minim veniam, quis nostrud exerci tation ullamcorper suscipit lobortis nisl ut aliquip ex ea commodo consequat. Duis autem vel eum iriure dolor in hendrerit in vulputate velit esse molestie consequat, vel illum dolore eu feugiat nulla facilisis at vero eros et accumsan et iusto odio dignissim qui blandit praesent luptatum zzril delenit augue duis dolore te feugait nulla facilisi.

Figure 5.57

Lorem ipsum dolor sit amet

consectetuer adipiscing elit, sed diam
nonummy nibh euismod tincidunt ut laoreet
dolore magna aliquam erat volutpat. Ut wisi
enim ad minim veniam, quis nostrud exerci
tation ullamcorper suscipit lobortis nisl ut
aliquip ex ea commodo consequat. Duis autem
vel eum iriure dolor in hendrerit in vulputate
velit esse molestie consequat, vel illum dolore
eu feugiat nulla facilisis at vero eros et
accumsan et iusto odio dignissim qui blandit
praesent luptatum zzril delenit augue duis
dolore te feugait nulla facilisi.

Figure 5.58

By the time the viewport window reaches 531 pixels wide or less, the layout completely breaks down **(Figure 5.58)**. At this point, if you have already handed your
files off to the front-end developer, they are going to come back to you and ask

what to do with the visual design in smaller viewports. Worse, the front-end developer could make the visual design decisions for you that change the layout when necessary, but potentially alienating the client! This will cost you time, goodwill, money, and future work.

All of this can be avoided by sketching out a simple wireframe at the desktop sized layout and using the evaluation template along with sample content to create a quick facsimile that you can view in the browser, on real devices to determine the optimal layout across a range of sizes. As you resize the viewpoint, watch for when the images become too hard to identify the necessary details. At that point, either fork the pen, or duplicate the HTML and CSS files on your computer and make another layout designed for a smaller viewport based on your wireframes. In **Figure 5.59**, I created a new layout once the viewport was at 854 pixels wide.

Figure 5.59

To ensure that you remember the viewport size you created the layout shift at, you can go into your layout program and create a new artboard at that size. I'd make an artboard at 854 pixels wide based on what's demonstrated in **Figure 5.59**. Another way to save this information is to add it directly to your pen or HTML/CSS files. Simply add the following code to your CSS and replace the max-width: 856px;

with whatever the pixel width of your viewport is **(Figure 5.59)**. By doing this, you are limiting how wide your layout will be. This way it can't be upsized and therefore you end up forgetting the ideal width range for this version of the layout. This CSS will also center the layout in the screen replicating what this layout could potentially look like in much larger screens if you don't create an optimized version for bigger screens **(Figure 5.60)**.

```
body {
    margin: 0 auto;
    max-width: 856px;
    width: 100%;
}
```

Figure 5.60

TIPS
Don't just rely on resizing the browser window on a larger sized screen for this exercise. While this is a good place to start, you need to view your choices on actual smartphone and tablet devices. This will ensure that your visual design choices are 100% accurate.

Evaluating a Page's Performance

Just as with your typographic choices, your layout—more specifically your choices on how to incorporate images into your layouts—can dramatically affect if a user engages with the website you are designing. Webpages loaded with images and fonts take a long time until the visitor sees the first view. Making the site's visitors wait for content will drive them away. Fortunately, performance is something you can test for before you begin the visual design process.

Using the layout from the previous section—assuming you optimized your images for the web—you almost have all the information that you need to run a performance test. To finish readying your evaluation template for performance testing, you need to add in enough typographic content to demonstrate your font choices and load the fonts you plan on using in your faux layouts. To begin to do this either fork your pen or duplicate the demo from the previous section one more time.

Working in the new pen or with the new files, copy the headline and first two paragraphs from the *Typographic Hierarchy Page - Template* and paste it into the HTML editor in CodePen or your index.html file in Brackets or used this finished pen https://codepen.io/browsersdevicesfonts/pen/NMreXx. Once you have added the content, you can now load your fonts. For this demonstration—and for practice—you need to load one headline font and a body font along with an italic and bold font from either Google Fonts or Typekit. This will give you four fonts total. Combined with the images already loaded, you should have a good indication of a potential webpage's performance. Be sure to use the <b> and the <i> tags in your HTML files. Even if you load the fonts via CSS, the browser is smart enough to not download fonts that are not utilized in the HTML document. You can review Chapter 04 *Typography* to refresh your memory on how to use web fonts if necessary. Once you have loaded the fonts, your layout should look very similar to **Figures 5.61 & 5.62**.

1280 × 533

consectetuer adipiscing elit, sed diam nonummy nibh euismod tincidunt ut laoreet dolore magna aliquam erat volutpat. Ut wisi enim ad minim veniam, quis nostrud exerci tation ullamcorper suscipit lobortis nisl ut aliquip ex ea commodo consequat. Duis autem vel eum iriure dolor in hendrerit in vulputate velit esse molestie consequat, vel illum dolore eu feugiat nulla facilisis at vero eros et accumsan et iusto odio dignissim qui blandit praesent luptatum zzril delenit augue duis dolore te feugait nulla facilisi.

Introduction to web typography

Web typography refers to the use of fonts on the *World Wide Web*. When HTML was first created, font faces and styles were controlled exclusively by the settings of each Web browser. There was no mechanism for individual Web pages to control font display until Netscape introduced the `<font>` tag in 1995, which was then standardized in the HTML 2 specification. However, the font specified by the tag had to be installed on the user's computer or a fallback font, such as a browser's default sans-serif or monospace font, would be used. The first **Cascading Style Sheets** specification was published in 1996 and provided the same capabilities.

Figure 5.61

```
HTML                                    CSS
capabilities.</p>                       @import url('https://fonts.googleapis.com/css?family=Exo+2:300,300i,600|Vollkorn:700');
  </div>
</div>                                   body {
                                          font-family: 'Exo 2', sans-serif;
                                          font-weight: 300;
                                        }

                                        i, em {
                                          font-style: italic;
                                        }

                                        b, strong {
                                          font-weight: 600;
                                        }

                                        h1, h2, h3 {
                                          font-family: 'Vollkorn', serif;
                                          font-weight: 700;
                                        }

                                        /* STOPIIIIII! DO NOT DELETE OR CHANGE ANYTHING BELOW THIS LINEIIIIII! */
```

1280 × 4

ntroduction to web typography

typography refers to the use of fonts on the *World Wide Web*. When HTML was first created, font faces and styles were controlled exclusively by the settings of each W vser. There was no mechanism for individual Web pages to control font display until Netscape introduced the `<font>` tag in 1995, which was then standardized in the H ecification. However, the font specified by the tag had to be installed on the user's computer or a fallback font, such as a browser's default sans-serif or monospace fon

Figure 5.62

What to Look For

Once you have uploaded your files to the performance test server and run the WebPage Test covered in Chapter 03 *Getting Started*, you can start to evaluate the results.

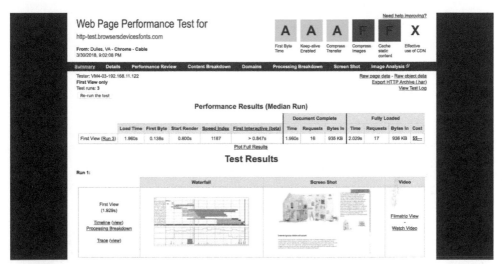

Figure 5.63

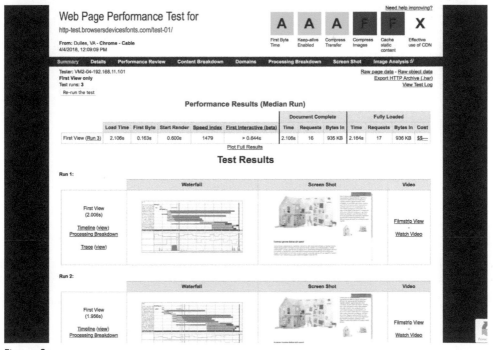

Figure 5.64

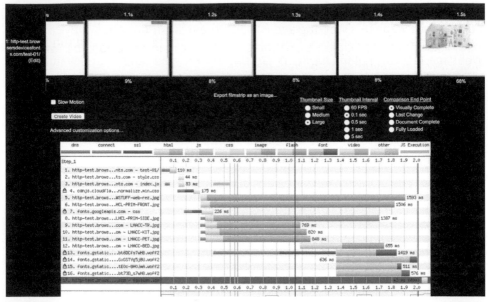

Figure 5.65

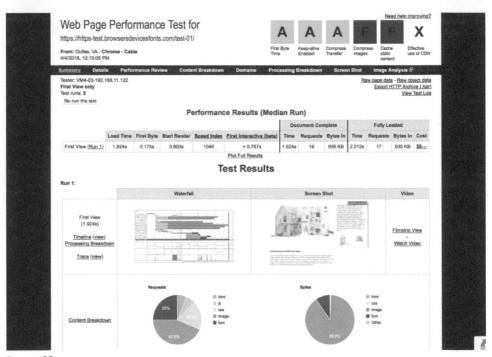

Figure 5.66

As you can see in **Figures 5.63 & 5.64** the evaluation page was served via HTTP from the performance test server, and the exact same files seen in **Figures 5.65 & 5.66** were served via HTTP2 from the performance test server with very different results. At first glance, 2.106 seconds vs. 1.924 seconds for the load time isn't very different. But remember, you have 1 second to give a website's visitor the impression that the website is working and will give them the information they came looking for. Thus, the load time isn't the critical piece of information, the *Time Till First View* is what you want to evaluate.

By clicking on the "Film Strip" view link on the results page, you bring up a 10th of a second snapshot timeline of what the website's visitor will see **(Figures 5.64 & 5.66)**, along with a timeline chart showing what is being loaded, in what order it's being loaded, how long it takes to start loading, and how long it takes to fully load. As you can see the HTTP server takes 1.5 seconds to deliver the first view to the visitor **(Figure 5.65)**. The HTTP2 server takes only .8 seconds to deliver the first view of the same exact files to the site's visitor **(Figure 5.67)**. That's over a half second quicker when the content is delivered by HTTP2, so it's important to make sure your client is using the technology that best delivers their content to the website's visitors.

Remember, it's not how long it takes the entire site to load that drives visitors away. Rather, visitors want to perceive that the website is working and will deliver them what they are looking for within a second, a goal that was achieved via HTTP2 demonstrated in **Figure 5.67**. If you run a test and find that your visual design choices are taking excessively long until first view, make sure your images are sized appropriately. If they aren't, resize them, if they are try reducing the number of images used on the page. You can also use systems fonts instead of custom loaded web fonts. If you are still having trouble, consider reaching out to your front-end developer to ask for strategies to make your visual designs more performant, before you continue to create visual mockups that could potentially have performance issues.

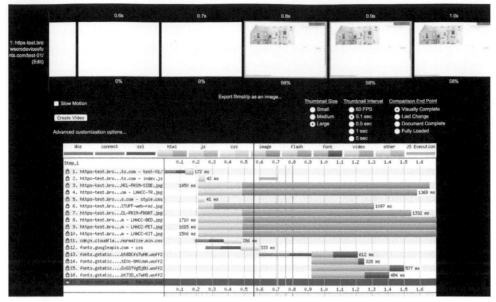

Figure 5.67

What I have just demonstrated to you may seem more on the front-end development side of the overall design process, and the front-end developer will make
more recommendations on how to load images, and other performance issues.
However, the visual design choices are yours to make. By incorporating the performance evaluation template into your workflow, you can be certain that your
visual design choices load relatively quickly.

6 Style Guides for Everyone

Unless you are a solo freelance visual designer and front-end developer, you will be working with other professionals to produce a live website. Whether you are a senior designer at an agency handing off your work to production designers and front-end developers, or a freelance visual designer handing off your visual mockups to a front-end developer, you are always working in a team.

Just like in the pre-interactive design days—unless you personally owned a letter-press, silkscreen equipment, or a 2 or 4 color printing press—you had to prepare instructions for your visual design choices for someone else to produce.

In fact, the production process for a website parallels that of the pre-computer days where a symphony of experts came together to produce the design piece. Much like today's post-print only world, pre-computer design production was a major undertaking requiring lots of different professions: such as a paste-up artist, typesetter, pre-press technician, press operator, in addition to the designer. Post-computer, sending a .pdf file to a printer made the production of design more straightforward. This ease of design production made available by the release of Aldus Pagemaker 1.0 in July 1985 has left many visual designers unprepared for the much more complex production process of interactive and web design.

As I have demonstrated throughout this book, simply giving a production designer or front-end developer a Sketch or Xd file with a few artboards doesn't give them all the information they will need. In order to get the most accurate representa-tion of your visual designs in live code; you need to provide whoever is next in line to receive your visual design files accurate details for reproduction. Fortunately, this step can be a seamless part of your workflow by compiling the evaluations and tests demonstrated throughout this book into a comprehensive style guide for the front-end developer.

Style Guides vs. Design Systems

Before you jump into compiling all your evaluations and tests into a style guide for the front-end developer, it's important to discuss what your final deliverables will be. While you may be visually designing a website, you are not designing every page of the website! If you look at modern websites you will notice content will vary from page to page, but the visual layout remains consistent. When it's all said and done, even if a website has hundreds of pages, there may be as little as three distinctly unique page layouts for the differing content types. The simplest example is an e-commerce website. The site will have a home page, a product cat-egory page, and a single product description page. Therefore, there is no need for the visual designer to physically mockup in Sketch or Xd every single page of an e-commerce website. Instead you will supply mockups of different page templates that the client will populate with content using a CMS like Shopify or WordPress. Those page mockups become a guide for the front-end developer to start work.

Designers—print or interactive—should be familiar with style guides. Most design programs have their students create a brand identity guide outlining the color palette and font choices. The brand identity guide will also demonstrate the proper use of a logo, and other images. More advanced brand identity guides may include a grid structure as well. As the industry moves towards designing inside out by creating elements that will be applied to a grid composing a page, there isn't enough information in a traditional style guide for the developer to work with. Instead of style guides, the interactive design industry has shifted to creating much more comprehensive *design systems*.

Design systems include everything that you normally find in traditional identity or style guides such as a logo's use, font choices, color palettes, grid structure, but add much more. For example, a comprehensive design system will include information on breakpoints, iconography, commonly used CSS declarations, and visual mockups of elements not currently part of the visual design that could be added when need arises in the future. Since there is already documentation readily available for creating design systems—sticking with the theme of this book—I'm going to demonstrate how to compile the existing evaluations and tests now part of your regular design workflow.

For a comprehensive explanation of design systems, I highly recommend that you read Brad Frost's book Atomic Design and subsequent resource Pattern Lab and check out the design system archive at https://styleguide.io.

Creating a Design System

A front-end developer's role is to bring your static mockups and clickable prototypes to life via HTML, CSS and JavaScript where necessary. However, even if you use the techniques I've outlined in this book, you are still unwittingly leaving interpretation of the visual design decisions up to the developer if you don't properly document your design choices. So, what exactly do you need to hand off to the developer? The following is a checklist with descriptions outlining how each piece of your design system helps the front-end developer.

Static Mockup

What I refer to as the "Static Mockup" is nothing more than your visual design in layout programs such as Bohemian Coding's Sketch. This file will be the primary source of information for your front-end developer unless you create a comprehensive Pattern Lab with production level HTML and CSS. Keeping in mind that you aren't designing every page of a website, rather templates for different content types, your mockup will generally contain only a few full-page layouts.

Remember, even though you don't have to design every page of the website, you do need to design each page template. Meaning, if you have three distinct content type pages for the site you need three distinct artboards to start with. Based on the layout evaluation techniques you learned in Chapter 05 *Finding Breakpoints for Text & Images*, you should also design multiple artboards for a single template page based on breakpoints. Basically, if you have three distinct template pages, you will also need to design a range of screen size variations from small to extra-large. You can expect to have to design each page's extremes—mobile and desktop—then anywhere from one to four extra pages based on breakpoints which were demonstrated in Chapter 05.

In addition to the individual content page templates, static mockups should contain information common in most Style Guides and Identity Systems including:

- Color palette, and any specific rules for the application of your color choices.

- Proper logo use, including spacing from other elements, proper display over images and color fields, etc.

- Font choices in context demonstrating the most common typographic HTML elements: H1–H6, P, EM, STRONG, UL, and OL.

- Example of the grid structure, i.e., 12 column, 16 column, etc. **(Figure 6.1)**. This should also have a clearly defined horizontal rhythm. Horizontal spacing between major sections of content on a page is just as important as the vertical gutter width but is often overlooked by the designer.

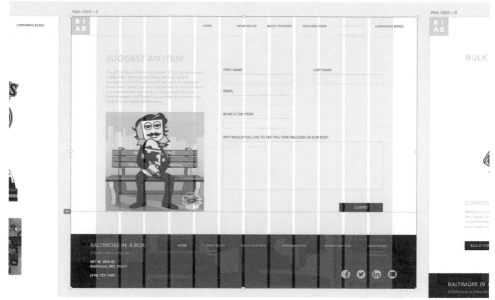

Nicole Rohrer "Baltimore in a Box" website mockup.

Figure 6.1

If you want to give your front-end developer a *Design System*, not just a *Style Guide* you will need to include additional visual information. Perhaps the most important is a comprehensive list of the different elements that are currently being used throughout the website, and elements that may be used in the future **(Figures 6.2 and 6.3)**. Elements that you should be designing can include:

• Buttons and Toggles

• Search and Form Fields

• Images Sliders

• Media Players

• Icon Sets

• Charts and Tables

• Navigation

• Links

• Modals, Popups, etc.

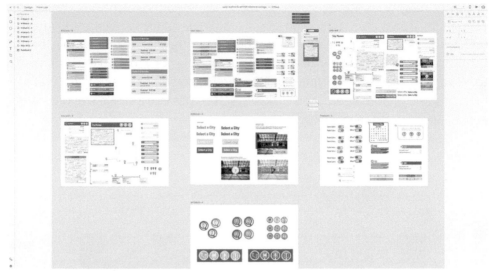

Kelly Stelmack "Your Stop" Element Collage

Figure 6.2

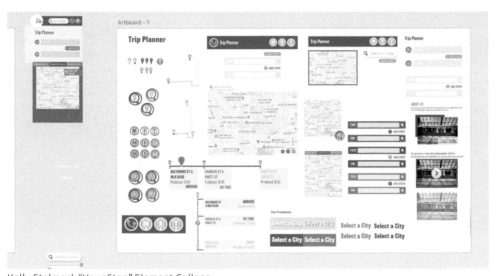

Kelly Stelmack "Your Stop" Element Collage

Figure 6.3

It's also the purview of the graphic designer to design the different micro interactions that will be used throughout the site. Micro interactions can include
mouse hover effects, the animation of drop-down menus opening, how content
moves into the page, and much, much more. With CSS's ability to perform complex
animations without the use of additional programming languages, micro interactions can greatly enhance the usability of a website without affecting its performance.

There are many ways that you can demonstrate how you want elements and page content to be animated. Animation specific tools like Adobe's Animate and After Affects can get the job done. There are programs on the market geared specifically towards micro interactions like Flinto and Principle. New tools like InVision's Studio and Anima App's Timeline plugin for Sketch combine the ability to create mockups, micro interactions, and clickable prototypes into a single workflow and are being released almost daily.

No matter the tools you choose, it's important for the visual designer to provide the front-end developer information on how elements within a page should be animated. **Figures 6.4–6.7** are stills from a demo I gave my students on creating micro interactions using Adobe After Effects. In this instance I animated an expanding/collapsing menu.

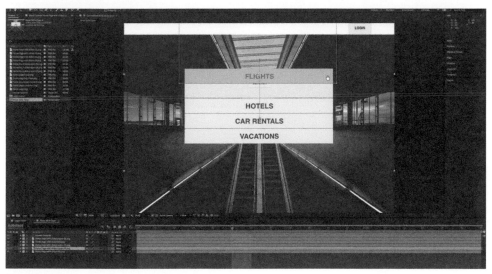

Figure 6.4

Figure 6.5

Figure 6.6

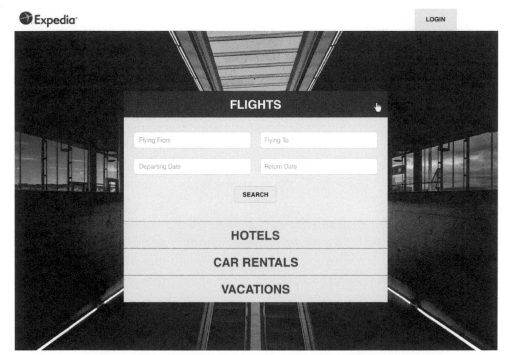

Figure 6.7

The purpose of creating examples of micro interactions, besides being the purview of the visual designer, also serves the purpose of demonstrating to the client your visual design intent. You may be able to verbally describe the micro interaction you are envisioning to your front-end developer by showing existing examples on websites or from places like CodePen. However, this isn't a professional approach to getting client buy in. By creating a detailed movie that demonstrates the animation style that will be a part of a site's design system, you are leaving out any ambiguity with the final deliverable to client.

Typographic Hierarchy Design System

Sticking with the architect, builder, blueprint analogy, to ensure the most accurate representation of her mockups, an architect would also build the physical structure herself. While not practical and requiring a lot of additional training for our architect to pull off, there are some things she could do with minimal experience such as nailing framing together or hanging drywall. HTML and CSS for graphic designers is no different, which I started to demonstrate in the "Hierarchy" section of Chapter 04 *Typography*. You could simply use the tools that I provided you in that chapter to make sure your static mockups are as accurate as possible, or you could build out the typographic foundation for your entire site. By building out the rest of the Typographic Hierarchy Page and turning it into a system, you will be handing off production level CSS code to your developer that will only need minor tweaking if any at all.

To fully build out the page either fork the Typographic Hierarchy Page – Template pen at https://codepen.io/browsersdevicesfonts/pen/YLqozx or download the template from the companion website at https://browsersdevicesfonts.com/exer-cise-files/06-typographic-hierarchy-page-template.zip. Whether you are using the Browser or Native Application based workflow, the HTML and CSS I will cover are the same for both methods. If you are using Brackets simply mimic the HTML and CSS that you see demonstrated in the screenshots from CodePen.

First, you will want to load at least four fonts—headline, regular, regular italic, and bold. You can also load a sub headline and a monospaced font. Just remember the more fonts you load into your design, the longer the site will take to download and render. You can see that I loaded Exo and Vollkorn from Google Fonts **(Figure 6.8)**. You can either follow along using the fonts I picked or choose your own.

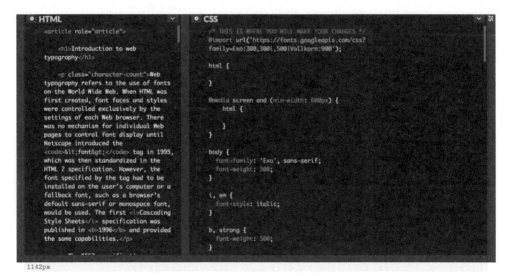

1142px

Introduction to web typography

Web typography refers to the use of fonts on the World Wide Web. When HTML was first created, font faces and styles were controlled exclusively by the settings of each Web browser. There was no mechanism for individual Web pages to control font display until Netscape introduced the <font> tag in 1995, which was then standardized in the HTML 2 specification. However, the font specified by the tag had to be installed on the user's computer or a fallback font, such as a browser's default sans-serif or monospace font, would be used. The first *Cascading Style Sheets* specification was published in **1996** and provided the same capabilities.

The CSS2 specification was released in 1998 and attempted to improve the font selection process by adding font matching, synthesis and download. These

Figure 6.8

Now that you've given the browser instructions on what fonts to load and where to load from, it's time to apply them. Remember, the browser is smart and won't download the font unless it sees that it's being applied in the CSS document. To apply the fonts, update your CSS to the following (change to reflect the font you chose). Also note, I changed the default Monospaced font to macOS's Menlo. Now-adays, most monospaced operating system fonts are designed much better than the default chosen by the browsers so it's good practice to make this update even if your client doesn't need the monospaced font since there is no performance hit using a system font.

```
body {
    background-color: #fff;
    font-color: #262626;
    font-family: 'Exo', sans-serif;
    font-weight: 300;
}

i, em {
    font-style: italic;
}

b, strong {
    font-weight: 500;
}

code {
    font-family: "Menlo", monospace;
}

h1, h2, h3, h4, h5, h6 {
    font-family: 'Vollkorn', serif;
    font-weight: 900;
}
```

Now that you've applied the new font choices, it's time to set the default font size of the entire HTML document. By default, the browser will set the font size to 16px. Generally, this is too small, especially for long form reading on a smart-phone. Taking a mobile first approach, I'm going to set the default font size to 20 pixels by adding the following CSS declaration.

```
html {
    font-size: 20px;
    line-height: 1.4;
}
```

Since this is a "Mobile First" approach , meaning that I'm making my visual design choices first on my mobile device, you will need to look at your page on a device from your device lab to ensure that your choices are correct **(Figure 6.9)**. Remember, if you are using a different font than I am, your values will be different. Again, there is no best practices value to set your default font size to. It's your job as the visual designer to do what is easiest for the site's visitor to read.

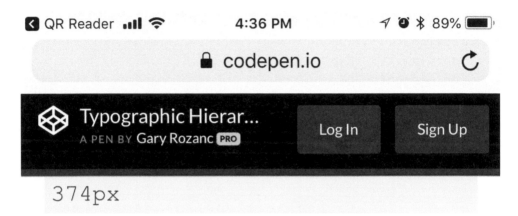

Figure 6.9

Once you have determined the best default font size for small screen devices, you need to check that the new default font size works on larger screens. As you can clearly see **(Figure 6.10)** the character counter is showing on the larger screen that using the optimal default font size for small screen devices is way too small for long form reading on a larger screen. Fortunately, thanks to the CSS @media rule you can give the web browser multiple sets of instructions based on screen size.

Introduction To Web Typography

Web typography refers to the use of fonts on the World Wide Web. When HTML was first created, font faces and styles were controlled exclusively by the settings of each Web browser. There was no mechanism for individual Web pages to control font display until Netscape introduced the <font> tag in 1995, which was then standardized in the HTML 2 specification. However, the font specified by the tag had to be installed on the user's computer or a fallback font, such as a browser's default sans-serif or monospace font, would be used. The first *Cascading Style Sheets* specification was published in **1996** and provided the same capabilities.

The CSS2 specification was released in 1998 and attempted to improve the font selection process by adding font matching, synthesis and

Figure 6.10

To change the size of the default font for larger screens while leaving the default size the same for smaller screens, add the following CSS media rule and declaration to the CSS panel in CodePen or style.css file in Brackets.

```
@media screen and (min-width: 1300px) {
    html {
        font-size: 34px;
    }
}
```

By adding the CSS above, you are giving the web browser a set of conditions of when to apply the CSS declarations. By adding @media screen and (min-width: 1300px) {…} rule you are telling the web browser if the viewport (open browser window) is 1300 pixels wide or wider change the font size applied to the HTML tag to 34 pixels and change the line height to 1.3. Once you have added the CSS check to see if the change in font size optimizes the line length for long form reading.

```
● HTML                                              ▽    ● CSS                                                     ▽  JS
          </h4>                                              /* THIS IS WHERE YOU WILL MAKE YOUR CHANGES */
         <p class="overflow"><code>@font-face           @import url('https://fonts.googleapis.com/css?family=Exo:300,300i,500|Vollkorn:900');
      {<br>
             font-family: 'Journal';                   html {
     src:url('http://your-                                   font-size: 20px;
     own.site/fonts/journal/journal.woff')                   line-height: 1.4;
     format('woff'),<br>                                 }
             url('http://your-
     own.site/fonts/journal/journal.svg#Journal')        @media screen and (min-width: 600px) {
     format('svg'),<br>                                      html {
          url('http://your-
     own.site/fonts/journal/journal.ttf')                    }
     format('truetype'),<br>                             }
          url('http://your-
     own.site/fonts/journal/journal.eot'),<br>           @media screen and (min-width: 1300px) {
          url('http://your-                                  html {
     own.site/fonts/journal/journal.eot?#iefix')             font-size: 34px;
     format('embedded-opentype');<br>                        line-height: 1.3;
          font-weight: normal;<br>                          }
          font-style: normal;<br>                        }
```

1312px

Introduction To Web Typography

Web typography refers to the use of fonts on the World Wide Web. When HTML
was first created, font faces and styles were controlled exclusively by the settings
of each Web browser. There was no mechanism for individual Web pages to control
font display until Netscape introduced the **<font>** tag in 1995, which was then
standardized in the HTML 2 specification. However, the font specified by the tag had

```
Console   Assets   Comments   ✖               Last saved less than a minute ago ⌐ | Delete | Share | Export | Embed | Collections    ▼
```

Figure 6.11

You can see that the optimal line length is right where it needs to be **(Figure 6.11)**.
Remember, the 45–75 character count range is a recommendation, not a rule. As
a visual designer, it's your job to determine the optimal readability based on the
font. Now that you've determined an optimal default font size for small screens,
and the other extreme large screens, it's time to determine if you need to make
any further adjustments. Simply resize the browser window and look for when the
character counter highlight is entirely on the first line towards the beginning or
middle of the line or moves to the second line. Once you determine when the optimal reading length breaks, create a new breakpoint (@media rule) based on the
width of the open window displayed in the upper left-hand corner of the screen. I
finally arrived at the following CSS @media rules.

```
@media screen and (min-width: 600px) {
    html {
        font-size: 24px;
    }
}


@media screen and (min-width: 960px) {
    html {
        font-size: 28px;
```

```
        line-height: 1.3;
    }
}


@media screen and (min-width: 1300px) {
    html {
        font-size: 34px;
        line-height: 1.3;
    }
}
```

Again, if you picked different fonts than I did, your values may be different than mine. Even if you picked the same fonts I did, you may find that you have a different visual preference than I do. It's for this exact reason that even though this part of the design system is optional, it's better for you to make these decisions rather than leave them up to your front-end developer to interpret from your static mockups.

Since I generally like to work from top to bottom, next we will style the <h1>–<h6> tags. I already covered what you should be looking for visually when styling the <h> tags in Chapter 04 *Typography*. You may want to review the "Evaluating & Testing" section if this isn't fresh in your memory before moving ahead. In Chapter 04 *Typography* I showed you how to resize each of your <h> tags to be more legible for a website's visitor using the fixed unit px. For evaluation purposes, this is fine. For production purposes, this is a very bad practice. Since pixels are a fixed size, anything sized using pixels will remain that size. This makes it nearly impossible for someone with visual disabilities to resize the font to make it larger or smaller.

Additionally, by default the size of the displayed text wrapped in an <h> tag is directly proportional to the default font size. Therefore, if you use a fixed unit of measure for styling your <h> tags, it won't scale in proportion with the default font size. To overcome this, you are going to use the flexible sizing unit em. Since em's are scaled based on the font size of their containing element, they are much better for production code versus pixels. By using em units instead of pixels, the <h> tags with font sizes styled in em will scale as the default font size changes. This means if done correctly, your <h> tags will change size as the @media rule changes the default font size. Add the following CSS as a starting point.

```css
h1, h2, h3, h4, h5, h6 {
    font-family: 'Vollkorn', serif;
    font-weight: 900;
    line-height: 1;
    text-transform: capitalize;
}

h1 {
    font-size: 2.5em;
}

h2 {
    font-size: 2.5em;
    margin: 1.25em 0 0 0;
     text-transform: uppercase;
}

h3 {
    font-size: 1.75em;
    margin-bottom: 0;
    text-decoration: underline;
}

h4 {
    font-size: 1.45em;
    margin-bottom: 0;
}

h2 + p, h3 + p,
h4 + p, h5 + p,
h6 + p {
    margin-top: 0;
}

h5, h6 {
    font-size: 1em;
    margin-bottom: 0;
}
```

```
h6 {
    font-family: 'Exo', sans-serif;
    font-weight: 500;
}
```

The only thing different in the code demonstrated above from what was covered in Chapter 04 *Typography* was the use of the flexible em units. Again, you will need to adjust these sizes to suit the font choices that you made if you didn't follow my examples **(Figure 6.12)**.

Figure 6.12

Now that you've added these additional styles, be sure to check your visual design choices using your device lab and by resizing the browser window on a larger screen **(Figures 6.13–6.15)**. You want to look for points where the sizing of the <h> tags breaks, just like you did with the default font size. When you do find a spot

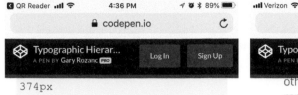

Typographic Hierar... ⠀ Log In ⠀ Sign Up ⠀⠀⠀⠀**Typographic Hierar...** ⠀ Log In ⠀ Sign Up
A PEN BY Gary Rozanc PRO ⠀⠀⠀⠀⠀⠀⠀⠀⠀⠀⠀⠀⠀⠀⠀⠀A PEN BY Gary Rozanc PRO

374px

Introduction To Web Typography

Web typography refers to the use of fonts on the World Wide Web. When HTML was first created, font faces and styles were controlled exclusively by the settings of each Web browser. There was no mechanism for individual Web pages to control font display until Netscape introduced the `<font>` tag in 1995, which was then standardized in the HTML 2 specification. However, the font specified by the tag had to be installed on the user's computer or a fallback font, such as a browser's default sans-serif or monospace font, would be

other decorative properties, but still represent the specified character.

WEB FONTS

History

A technique to download remote fonts was first specified in the CSS2 specification, which introduced the `@font-face` rule.

It was (and remains[8]) controversial because using a remote font as part of a Web page allows the font to be freely downloaded. This could result in fonts being used against the terms of their license or illegally spread through the Web. TrueDoc (PFR) Embedded

⟨ ⟩ ⬆ ⬒ ⬓ ⠀⠀⠀⠀⠀⟨ ⟩ ⬆ ⬒ ⬓

Figure 6.13 ⠀⠀⠀⠀⠀⠀⠀⠀⠀⠀⠀⠀⠀⠀⠀⠀Figure 6.14

1240px

WEB FONTS

History

A technique to download remote fonts was first specified in the CSS2 specification, which introduced the `@font-face` rule.

It was (and remains[8]) controversial because using a remote font as part of a Web page allows the font to be freely downloaded. This could result in fonts being used against the terms of their license or illegally spread through the Web. TrueDoc (PFR) Embedded OpenType (EOT) and Web

Figure 6.15

where you need to make a visual design adjustment add a new @media rule. Based on the font choices I made for this demonstration, I decided it was necessary to add the new @media rule when the viewport is a minimum width of 1100 pixels.

```
@media screen and (min-width: 1100px) {
    h1 {
        font-size: 3.25em;
    }

    h2 {
        font-size: 2.65em;
     }
    h4 {
        font-size: 1.25em;
    }
}
```

It's also important to note that this @media rule, and all @media rules need to go under the CSS declaration it's meant to override.

```
@media screen and (min-width: 1100px) {
    h1 {
        font-size: 3.25em;
    }
}

h1 {
    font-size: 2.5em;
}
```

Using the code example above, if you were to write the following CSS in order from top to bottom the web browser would first read the @media rule and apply the font-size: 3.25em; to all <h1> tags with a minimum viewport width of 1100px since web browsers read files from top tp bottom. Next, the browser would read the next CSS <h1> declaration and style every single <h1> tag with a font-size: 2.5em; overriding the previous declaration. So, remember to follow the default CSS declarations with the @media rule that you want to override it with.

To practice putting @media rules in the proper order, and continue adjusting the default typographic styles, we will look at the HTML <sup>, <sub>, and <small>

tags. Depending on the x-height of your font, when marked up HTML the default superscript and subscript font size may be too big or too small. Based on the font choices I made for this demo, I decided to reduce the default sizing of these tags. However, after viewing my choices with my device lab I decided to add an @media rule to have two different <sup> and <sub> sizes. As for the order, try putting the @media rule for the <sup> and <sub> tags above the default CSS declaration and see how the browser responds.

```css
sup, sub {
    font-size: .75em;
}

@media screen and (min-width: 1100px) {
    sup, sub {
      font-size: .6em;
    }
}
```

It's also worth mentioning the <small> tag. Its semantic purpose for screen readers and search engines is to define the "small," or "fine print" such as legal disclaimers and copyright information. Again, the <small> tag is useful for SEO purposes, but depending on the font, and your visual design decisions, the default style of the tag may either be too big or too small. You can see how I adjusted mine for this demonstration below.

```css
small {
    font-size: .65em;
}
```

The last HTML element that adversely affects the visual representation of the content is the <dl> (Definition List) and its companion <dt> (Definition Term) and <dd> (Definition Description) elements. As you can see the definition descriptions are indented underneath the definition description **(Figure 6.16)**. With a short definition such as "Serif" it becomes really hard to tell where the definition starts. Making matters worse, the line-height between each line and each set of <dt> and <dd> tags makes the whole block of text look like an oddly indented paragraph.

Simply adding the following CSS declarations—adjusted for your own font choices—will make the definition list much easier to read **(Figure 6.17)**.

```css
dt {
    font-weight: 500;
}

dd {
    line-height: 1.25;
     margin: 0 0 .35em 0;
}
```

You are not limited to what I've just demonstrated and can get more creative with
the styling of your definition lists. However, to further adjust the visual layout of
the lists requires knowledge of CSS layout techniques which are beyond the scope
of this book. If you want more creative freedom with the visual styling of your
definition lists, it's best to create them in your static mockup and let your front-
end developer write the production code.

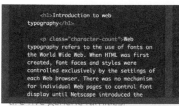

1240px

Sans-serif
Fonts that do not have decorative
considered easier to read on scre
Serif
Fonts that have decorative markir
Monospace
Fonts in which all characters are
Cursive
Fonts that resemble cursive writi
can be difficult to read at small s
Fantasy
Fonts that may contain symbols
snecified character

Figure 6.16

1240px
generic font families. These families are designed to split f
their general appearance. They are commonly specified as
as a last resort in the event that none of the fonts specifie
are five generic families:[6]

Sans-serif
Fonts that do not have decorative markings, or serifs, on tr
considered easier to read on screens.[7]

Serif
Fonts that have decorative markings, or serifs, present on

Monospace
Fonts in which all characters are equally wide.

Cursive

Figure 6.17

There are three other tags you should consider styling, even if they aren't currently being used in your designs **(Figure 6.18)**. The <address> tag is very useful for
helping search engines, but it also italicizes the address by default. One semantic
used of the <cite> tag is to cite a quote or phrase, or list cited materials such as
journal articles. In either case, the <cite> tag by default italicizes the marked-up

text. Finally, you have the <q> tag which is used to quote shorter statements and phrases. By default, it adds double quotes around the marked-up text. If this isn't desirable, you will need to work with your front-end developer to change the <q> tag's default styling.

```html
<p>
    1000 Hilltop Circle
    Baltimore, MD 21250
</p>

<address>
    1000 Hilltop Circle
    Baltimore, MD 21250
</address>

<div>
    <p>"There are three responses to a piece of design – yes, no, and WOW! Wow is the one to
aim for." <cite>Milton Glaser</cite></p>
    <p><q>"There are three responses to a piece of design – yes, no, and WOW! Wow is the one to
aim for."</q> <cite>Milton Glaser</cite>
</div>
```

1000 Hilltop Circle Baltimore, MD 21250

1000 Hilltop Circle Baltimore, MD 21250

"There are three responses to a piece of design – yes, no, and WOW! Wow is the one to aim for." *Milton Glaser*

""There are three responses to a piece of design – yes, no, and WOW! Wow is the one to aim for."" *Milton Glaser*

Figure 6.18

Another ancillary tag you may want to consider styling is the <figcaption> tag. Just like the name implies, the figcaption's purpose is to include supporting text for charts, photos, illustrations—basically all kinds of images outside of the main document flow. While there isn't any default styling applied, you may want to distinguish it visually from normal paragraph styling **(Figure 6.19)**.

Figure 6.19

Since it was already covered in-depth in Chapter 04 *Typography,* I'm only going to remind you to adjust your unordered and ordered lists. I've included the CSS declarations I used for reference. You may use these as a starting point and simply adjust the values as necessary.

```
ul {
    padding-left: 1em;
}

ol {
    list-style-type: decimal-leading-zero;
    margin-top: 0;
    padding-left: 2em;
}

ul li,
ol li {
    line-height: 1.25;
    margin-bottom: .3em;
}

p + ul,
p + ol {
    margin-top: -.9em;
}
```

Finally, there are quite a few other HTML tags that visually affect the typography on a web page. You may want to consider styling these as well on a case by case basis since most have very specific uses not used day to day.

- `<samp>`
- `<kbd>`
- `<var>`
- `<pre>`
- `<u>`
- `<s>` and `<del>`
- `<output>`

With a little more work, you have an excellent foundational typographic design system to add to your design system. It's worth the extra effort, not only because it removes any guess work by your front-end developer, it also is a boilerplate for all of your future projects! All you will need to do to use this on future projects is load new font choices and adjust the existing CSS values and media rules to best display your new font choices.

Clickable Prototype

In the end, your static mockups will serve two purposes. The first we already covered, blue-prints for your front-end developer. The second purpose is to create what I like to call "clickable prototypes" that you present to your client to demonstrate the user flow and visual design **(Figure 6.20)**. Adobe Xd, Bohemian Coding's Sketch, and InVision let you turn elements in your artboards into hot spots that when clicked take the user to another artboard of your design. I bring up the clickable prototype in this chapter because whichever layout program you choose, you want it to quickly and intuitively meet the demands of these two needs.

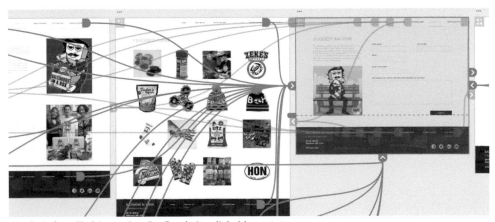

Nicole Rohrer "Baltimore in a Box" website clickable prototype
Figure 6.20

Bohemian Coding's Sketch can be used to create clickable prototypes for presenting to your client by uploading your artboards to the InVision app or work directly in Sketch with InVision's Craft plugin. The Craft and Zeplin plugins for Sketch also allow front-end developers to extract some base CSS styles from your static mockups. At the opposite end of the spectrum, Adobe's print design layout program InDesign doesn't easily import into InVision to create clickable prototypes or produce CSS styles usable by your front-end developer. So whichever layout program you choose for your design workflow, make sure that it meets the needs of not only you, but those of your client, and makes it easy for your front-end developer to extract the necessary information.

The Hand Off

Before you hand off the files to the front-end developer, you need to add some final documentation. Using the element collages as an example, your front-end developer won't have any idea what the elements are that aren't being used in the static mockup. Simply numbering the elements and creating a list somewhere in the file that briefly describes the use of the element will be enough information to keep the front-end developer from calling you unnecessarily.

Figure 6.21

You also need to label each artboard. Leaving the default name generated by the layout program will make it difficult for anyone working with your files to understand your intent **(Figures 6.21 & 6.22)**. You don't want to leave your front-end developer guessing! You should also clearly and consistently name and group your layers. If you struggle to select a text box, or border—and you use the program every day—think about your front-end developer who is trying to figure out the font size you picked, the thickness of a border, or the color of a background. Clearly naming and grouping content within the layers will help make the hunt for this information much easier. Giving your layers names that reflect the actual element is even more helpful. Consider giving detailed names such as "main-navigation", or "home-page-slider" to make your files easier to interpret.

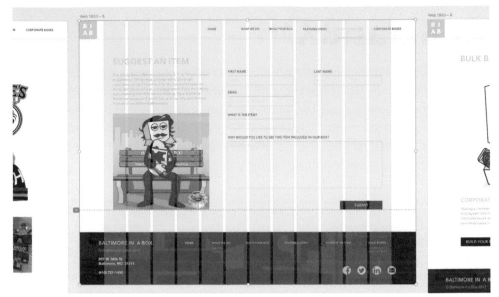

Figure 6.22

Finally, there is a multitude of standalone programs out there such as Abstract and InVision that make documenting your files a seamless part of your workflow. Sketch also has a number of third-party plugins for writing notes within the program. This is a good way to instruct a front-end developer to look at an animation that you may have created in a separate program. Even a spread-sheet with notes on specific artboard, elements, and micro interactions is helpful and will make it much easier for you to work with your front-end developer. Remember to document everything as clearly as you can to reduce or remove any possibility for miscommunication between you and the front-end developer or between you and your client!

Conclusion

When it comes time to hand off the files to your front-end developer remember to include the static mockups from your layout program of choice, movies or animated gifs of your micro interactions, your style tiles or mood boards, and element collages. When all these visual design blueprints are coupled with live code from your Typographic Hierarchy page and detailed documentation your front-end developer can accurately produce your visual design choices.

One last thought, the HTML and CSS demonstrated in this book is far from exhaustive. As a visual designer, you will still benefit from learning additional methods of producing live websites. Specifically, I highly recommend learning layout methods using CSS's Flexbox and Grid properties. These recent additions to the CSS specification give greater control over the display and placement of content in your HTML pages. The control designers now have greatly surpasses what was available just a few years ago. By exploring these new CSS specifications, you will have a greater understanding of the web as a medium and place yourself in a stronger position when competing for design jobs or freelance work.

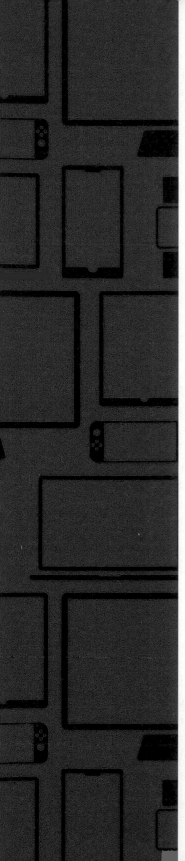

Index